GW00724741

DOING BED & BREAKFAST

DOING BED
& BREAKFAST

Audrey Vellacott
and Liz Christmas

DAVID & CHARLES
Newton Abbot   London   North Pomfret (Vt)

British Library Cataloguing in Publication Data

Vellacott, Audrey
  Doing bed and breakfast.
  1. Hotel management
  I. Title   II. Christmas, Liz
  647'.94   TX911.3.M27
  ISBN 0-7153-8236-5

© Audrey Vellacott and Liz Christmas 1982

All rights reserved. No part of this publication may be
reproduced, stored in a retrieval system, or transmitted, in any
form or by any means, electronic, mechanical, photocopying,
recording or otherwise, without the prior permission of
David & Charles (Publishers) Limited

Typeset by Typesetters (Birmingham) Ltd
and printed in Great Britain
by A. Wheaton & Co. Ltd, Hennock Road, Exeter
for David & Charles (Publishers) Limited
Brunel House Newton Abbot Devon

Published in the United States of America
by David & Charles Inc
North Pomfret Vermont 05053 USA

Contents

While every care has been taken to ensure the accuracy of the information contained in this book, the authors and publishers cannot accept responsibility for any error or omission.

Acknowledgements

The authors would like to thank the following for their help, which has been invaluable during the preparation of this book; Mrs E. M. Bottone, Sandra Cambridge, Martin Capon, Linda Christmas, Janet M. Clifford, the Consumers' Association for permission to quote from their *Home Safety Report*, Mrs S. J. Devon, the English Tourist Board for permission to reproduce the English Tourist Board Standards, Oliver Flavin, Mr D. G. Harbottle, Ellie Heard for understanding so well all our notes, Miss Jane E. King, Steve Kirby, Mr J. Langdon, John Male, Mary and Alastair Matthews, Mark Perry, Gilly and James Robertson, Mr A. Ritchie, Jennie Small for permission to refer to the findings of her unpublished report 'Tourists and their Hosts: A Socio-Psychological Analysis', Department of Psychology, University of Surrey, 1978, John Stanford of RADAR, Mr J. P. Stoneham, Miss K. C. C. Taylor, John and Nellie Thompson, Dr S. Woodman, Mr L. Farthing, and lastly John and Colin for their continual support.

1

Before You Begin

In many areas, even those well supplied with hotels, lower-priced Bed and Breakfast accommodation will always be needed to give visitors the comforts of home, good food and value for money. People enjoy a Bed and Breakfast holiday because it gives them the personal touch which larger hotels often find difficult to provide. By being guests in your home, they know that at the end of the evening they can settle into a comfortable bed and enjoy a nourishing breakfast the following morning. And for a short while they will have entered into your family life.

There are many reasons why people start having paying guests. It can be an ideal way to supplement the family income and be there when the children come home from school. Some-one living in a six-bedroomed house may decide to utilise the extra space. It could be redundancy money which has led to the chance of changing direction and beginning something afresh in a new area. Some people may simply have enjoyed their own Bed and Breakfast holidays so much that they would like to have guests to stay in their own home. It is, in fact, an ideal business for anyone who has confidence in their ability to make others welcome, and who will enjoy the company they bring. There is a lot of satisfaction to be had from the service one is providing.

We hope to give a good idea of how to begin your Bed and

Breakfast business and make it a success. We will not tell you the only way to go about it. There are as many ideas and opinions as there are landlords and landladies! But we have included enough to be able to say that if you go about it our way, you should not go out of business too quickly!

However, it is very important to consider the commitment involved in running this type of business. There is no point in just deciding to go ahead and see what happens. Your guests will demand a great deal of time, effort and attention, often to the detriment of your other interests and activities. You must stop and think of all the changes it will bring. The guests have to come first. It is no good keeping them waiting for breakfast while you feed the family. Everyone already in the house takes second place to the needs of those who have paid for your time and services, and as anyone already doing Bed and Breakfast will testify, there is a great deal of hard work involved, not to mention the sacrifices which have to be made by everyone else living in the house. And it is often these changes which people do not spend enough time considering. Have you enough time in the day to cater for visitors? A family with young children or a farming family will often have sufficient to keep them fully occupied, and one must therefore consider the additional cost in hours and energy spent on paying guests. On the other hand, those in the country often consider that any additional effort involved is more than compensated for by the company and friendship of their annual guests.

The most difficult change, for many people, is adjusting to the loss of privacy. This can be a shock if not prepared in advance. Previously, visitors would have knocked, or rung the bell, or even just shouted a greeting as they came in the front door. Now, guests will come in, go to their rooms and often not even acknowledge your existence! There will be activity in your home which is not any of your business, and you will have to merge very successfully into the background. Parts of your home belong to your guests. They have paid to be able to treat it as their home too, and you have to be able to give it over to them willingly. One must not mind too much if it gets damaged, or used in a way one does not approve of. A coat of paint always works wonders once the guests have gone. If you are unhappy about sharing your home, you are not likely to appreciate the guests very much.

You can cope with this to some degree by keeping a proportion of the living area in the house private and only for the family's use. The extent to which this is done is going to reflect your personality. Many of those taking guests are very willing to share every aspect of their day-to-day activity with them. Their guests are like 'paying friends'. They come into the kitchen and make tea whenever they feel like it, and join in with family activities in the evening. If you feel that is not the way it will work for you, and that there will have to be definite no-go areas, simply in order to escape from time to time, decide, before you have the first visitor, where your private rooms will be. Put 'Private' on the doors to discourage the guests, and make them aware of their limits. And do not be ashamed if you need to impose limits which the landlady or landlord nearby does not. You must give as much as possible to guests, but not so much that you are under stress and becoming crotchety! You have to run your business as it suits you.

Retaining one's privacy is especially important if there are children or teenagers in the family. They will be the ones who, most of all, resent the intrusion into their homes. Guests' children can take advantage of one's own children's toys etc., and, even although you are likely to reprimand them if it gets out of hand, one's children have to be able to share at least some of their possessions with others. Often they will have already given up their bedrooms for guests and have to be much quieter and more considerate than children are prone to be! Muttering 'F.H.B.' ('Family Hold Back') *sotto voce* when the children make demands will often remind them that the guests need your attention as much as they do, but by giving them a room which is theirs, where special toys and games can be kept and where family quarrels can be aired in private, you can help to alleviate some of the pressures they may feel.

They can also be made aware of the advantages of a constant stream of visitors. Their meals are likely to improve, either because they taste your attempts at new dishes, or because they will get what the guests eat. There will be other children to play with; especially valuable in country areas, where long holidays mean separation from school friends. And they may in the end be glad of the company, often looking forward to the arrival of the annual guests.

Never underestimate the amount of time which paying guests

will take. It is no good if you disappear into the kitchen to get on with the work every time they want to talk. They must get to know you too. Some guests will want to talk a lot, others will be happy with a few words, and it is important to recognise which ones will need to be entertained. When they come down for breakfast, you have to greet them, and chat for a minute, while planning breakfast in your head at the same time. Make them feel welcome, even though you have run out of eggs and the baby is howling!

You and your family must like people. You can think what you like about them in the privacy of your rooms, but tolerance and an ability to charm them are needed when dealing with them face to face. A sense of humour will be invaluable, and the ability to shrug off many things of which you may disapprove. If you are intolerant, rigid and happiest with your own company, do not do Bed and Breakfast!

As well as an awareness of guests and their needs, you will also need to have confidence in your ability to cook and a good business head for managing the finances and housekeeping. Initially it is a good idea to keep the numbers small, so that you can manage alone most of the time, giving guests your full attention. This will please them and it will not mean that there are too many to cope with before finding your feet. It will also give you a chance to find out if you like having paying guests in your home! In the beginning, there are bound to be a certain proportion of visitors who do not like the way the house is run. The first few years are always something of an experiment. But by starting as you mean to continue, and managing the home, above all, in a way which suits you and the family, you will find, in a year or two, that the guests who return are the ones who like the way you do things. Then there is a great feeling of progress. Do not try to please all the guests—it is impossible. Please yourself and the guests who suit you will return.

Decide, before taking visitors, whether any particular group of guests is likely to cause problems. If the house is small, there is little garden, and the thought of dog hairs on the furniture makes you cringe, do not take dogs! They need a lot of space and a responsible owner with them. Children, especially the under-fives, tend to dominate the dining-room, and wake up a lot at night in a strange house. On the other hand, you may love a house full of children and make them particularly welcome. This depends so much on your own attitude, family etc. Know yourself, your limits and tolerances, and begin as you hope to carry on. It is far better to say 'No' straight away, than endure a week or so of something you knew was not going to make you particularly happy!

Choosing Suitable Premises
If looking for a house from which to begin a Bed and Breakfast business, personal taste must come first. You may wish to stay in the area whose potential you know well, or you may consider moving. But there is little point in buying a property in town if you have always wanted to live and work in country surroundings, or vice versa. So an area in which you will enjoy working is the first consideration. Then think about the situation of the property. Will car parking be awkward if the house is in the town centre? Will guests ever find you five miles down a country lane? You are unlikely to pick up much passing trade if too far out of the way and it could take much longer to become established.

One must also consider whether to purchase a property to convert oneself or an established concern. Because of the expense involved in order to comply with the Fire Precautions Act, many people already doing Bed and Breakfast have had to decide whether it is worth keeping bedrooms for more than six visitors. For those possibly contemplating the purchase of a suitable property, the Fire Precautions Act must be borne in mind when deciding how many visitors the property will accommodate (see Chapter 2). If a Fire Certificate would be necessary, is there enough cash available to make the appropriate alterations, can you borrow enough, or can the price of the property be reduced accordingly?

Choose a house which is structurally sound and will not need a great deal of major renovation. Find out how much it will cost to insure as a business. Although many guests are attracted to thatched buildings, one usually has to pay a higher premium. If inexperienced at catering, ideally look for a house with three spare bedrooms, enabling you to cater for five or six people. Then if happy with taking in paying guests, see if the property can easily be altered to accommodate more visitors or increase facilities.

If you decide that a 'going concern' is preferable, and you would rather pay more for a property which is already 'purpose built', try to find out why the present proprietors are leaving. Is the house too isolated, or unattractive to visitors, or is it that they themselves and the business seem inefficient and badly organised (i.e. something which offers you scope for improvement)? Ask to see annual gas, electricity, fuel and rates bills in order to estimate running costs. As a prospective purchaser you may be entitled to see the audited accounts for the previous trading period, which will give you an indication of the weekly income and gross profits. And look carefully at decorations, furniture and fittings to assess whether they will need replacing in the near future.

Seasonal or All the Year Round

There is not much point in starting up and then finding out that no one comes to stay at all. One has to make sure that there is in fact a demand in the area for Bed and Breakfast. Obviously, if it is already well served with hotels and larger guest houses, with a well established tourist industry, it will not be very difficult to understand why people visit. There will always be in these areas a continual need for lower-priced, 'value-for-money' accommodation of the type you are considering providing. However, if every second house already does Bed and Breakfast you are going to have to provide a much better service, as the competition will be much fiercer. In the majority of tourist areas there is a very well defined holiday season, but there is now a growing demand for out of season holidays, as more and more people prefer to take their break away from the rush of the summer months. So, even though those nearby only do Bed and Breakfast in the summer, you may decide to fill the need for off-peak holidays. It is certainly easier, in the beginning, to spread the load over a longer time period, and have days when there are no guests in the house. You can even take the sign down! Summer-only visitors concentrate 'the business' into three or four months, but may leave one pretty exhausted at the end of it!

If not so accessible to the established tourist trade, you may have to look further afield for potential customers. In both the more remote country areas and the middle of towns and cities there is an increasing demand for more reasonably priced accommodation. Familiarise yourself with local attractions and activities. There may be field courses going on within the vicinity, a reservoir attracting fishermen during the coarse season, a nearby college running winter study courses, etc. These and other activities ensure visitors will be coming into the area, out of season and looking for somewhere to stay. The right advertising can mean a steady stream of guests more interested in 'specialist holidays'.

In very isolated spots, however, there may be times of the year when visitors could find it impossible to reach you by car or public transport. The cottage two miles along a farm track may be just the quiet autumn holiday for worn-out city visitors, but in the winter they will not thank you if the only way they can reach the nearest railway station is by negotiating the snowdrifts in the cab of the local farmer's four-wheel-drive tractor!

Bed, Breakfast and Evening Meal?

In many areas where there are cafés, restaurants, etc., and guests have a choice of where to eat out in the evening, the decision whether to provide an evening meal for the guests may be an easy one to make. If you enjoy cooking, and think that you will have the time and energy to cook every night, you will probably advertise 'Bed, Breakfast and Evening Meal'. But do remember that there is much more effort involved in the preparation of the evening meal than in breakfast alone and it is often difficult to charge a realistic price, taking into account both the cost of food and the time and labour involved. You are also much less free to spend the rest of the day as you wish. If planning Bed and

Breakfast only, guests will appreciate it if you can recommend reliable places where they can get a reasonable meal.

However, in many country areas visitors may not come for Bed and Breakfast only if they cannot have some kind of meal in the evening. Whereas they will be happy to fend for themselves during the day, having eaten a good breakfast, they will want something to eat in the evening without having to travel miles to the nearest restaurant. This is especially true of guests who are touring. Because much of the appeal of Bed and Breakfast is that it does not need to be booked too far in advance, many guests will be travelling to a further destination, and once they arrive they are likely to want a reasonable meal. If you cannot provide it in country areas, they may travel on until they find someone who will. In those circumstances, if one's inclinations and cooking ability do not extend to a full-scale dinner, one could simply offer a 'high-tea' type menu of fish and chips or salad, with bread, jam, cake and tea at a reasonable cost. The cost of the food should be approximately 50 per cent of the price charged.

Whereas most of the larger hotels are rather impersonal, and from the inside could be in any part of the country, there are a huge variety of types of houses doing Bed and Breakfast, each of which reflect something different of the occupants and locality. By opening your home to visitors, even for a short time, and extending hospitality to them, you will be giving them an insight into your way of life. Because they share so much with you, doing Bed and Breakfast must therefore be the decision of everyone in the family.

2

Requirements and Regulations

There is legislation affecting a Bed and Breakfast business which must be considered before beginning. It can be rather daunting, but most of it exists for the benefit of proprietor and guests. Although much of the legislation is similar throughout the United Kingdom, it could differ slightly in Scotland and Northern Ireland, so do consult the appropriate authority.

Planning Permission

Bed and Breakfast done in a minor way, using one or two spare rooms in the house and for a small part of the year, is unlikely to require planning permission. This is the way in which most people start taking paying guests. The visitors occupy spare bedrooms and share the family's facilities, with the landlord or landlady coping alone, but they are not the major source of income for the household.

However, if one decides to make more of the house available to a larger number of guests and increase guest facilities, this could be considered a 'material change of use' of the property by the local Planning Department. The guests would be staying in a small 'guest house' and the owners probably seen to have a much more commercial attitude to the 'business'.

The scale of the undertaking will depend to a great extent on the size of the property: there may be only one or two spare rooms and only a few paying guests could stay at any time. However, if you live in a large house or are contemplating purchasing one, hoping to fill it with Bed and Breakfast visitors, planning permission will be required. Large-scale catering could also lead to your home being considered as a small 'guest house'. Bed and Breakfast only may be all right, but the additional provision of an evening meal may suggest a more commercial concern.

Each case, however, is always considered on its own merits, because 'material change of use' is a difficult term to define. The local Planning Office will welcome an informal approach to them if you have any doubts about the scale of your business.

Whatever the size of the property, the Planning Office will want to know where the guests are going to park their cars. Do not assume that they will be able to park in front of the house. You and your visitors have no more right in law to park outside your home than anyone else. The fact that it is done so often is only due to the courtesy of neighbours and ultimately the police, who do have the right to move cars on, or even paint yellow lines on the road if there are continual obstructions! One is not going to be very popular with neighbours if they return from work and find themselves unable to park in their usual space because of your guests' cars. And their continual complaints may suggest to the local Planning Office that the house is being used often enough by paying guests for 'change of use' to be applicable. Adequate safe parking within walking distance should be provided for guests' cars.

Fire Precautions and Building Regulations

A Fire Certificate is required if there is sleeping accommodation for more than six persons, including staff, or if one is providing any sleeping accommodation above the first floor or below the ground floor. If premises require a Fire Certificate the owners must apply to the Fire Authority, although they can continue the business from the time of application until the Fire Authority either grant or refuse to grant a Fire Certificate. The Fire Prevention Officer will inspect the premises shortly after application and outline the necessary measures to be taken, giving a time limit for the work (which may be extended if necessary). It is likely that there will have to be a fire alarm system, fire-resistant and self-closing doors, fire extinguishers and a secondary lighting system, but each local authority can interpret the legislation in different ways. Your local Fire Prevention Officer is the best person to advise. A Fire Certificate will be granted once all the alterations have been seen to be made.

Financial help may come from the bank manager or from the local authority, many of which make loans for fire precautions work.

Guests are much more conscious nowadays of fire safety and may well ask, on booking, if there is a Fire Certificate for the building. Even if you are not required to comply with the Act it is wise to take some basic fire precautions. Smoking in bedrooms, leaving television sets plugged in at night and chip pan fires are among the major causes of house fires. A basic fire alarm system, fire-resistant doors and the provision of fire blankets and extinguishers will mean that you are more prepared to cope in an emergency. As for guests, there should be notices in the bedrooms containing advice on what to do in the event of fire, including specific directions to an escape route. In Appendix C you will find an example of the type of notice you could display. The local Fire Prevention Officer will be very willing to come and give advice on these and other aspects of fire safety.

Any extensions or alterations to the buildings or to the drainage systems must comply with Government Building Regulations. Even adding a wash-hand basin in a bedroom constitutes an extra fitting and must have building approval.

The Planning Department, Fire Prevention Officer and the office responsible for Building Regulations often work very closely together, and a visit to one will keep you informed of any ways in which increasing your facilities for paying guests would require you to take advice from another department.

Mortgage or Tenancy Agreements and Rates

If you have a mortgage or are a tenant, it is necessary to examine the terms of the mortgage or tenancy agreement to see if it is permissible to carry on a 'business' from that address. On many modern building estates there are covenants (i.e. restrictions) which say that no trade or business may be carried on there. The tenancy agreement of a tenant farmer may also not allow him to take in Bed and Breakfast guests. In all these situations it may be possible to negotiate, and it is advisable to do so as early in your planning as possible.

It is unlikely that a small Bed and Breakfast business in your home which takes in paying guests for a short period of time each year would mean reassessment for rating purposes, although any structural alterations made to the property in the course of improving it may mean a rise in its rateable value. Such alterations would include extensions or addition of extra bedrooms or toilets, and the full or partial installation of central heating.

However, where a substantial number of rooms in the house are occupied all year round by paying guests, it is likely that the house will fall into the 'business' category. But the attitudes of the local rating authorities do vary, and it is best to clarify the position with the Valuation Officer before starting (see 'Inland Revenue—Valuation Officers' in the phone book).

Public Health and Hygiene

Guests coming into Bed and Breakfast accommodation want a freshly made bed in a clean room, with a good meal cooked in hygienic conditions—a high standard of cleanliness must always be maintained. The Food Hygiene Regulations apply to anyone owning, managing or carrying on a 'Food Business', i.e. where food is served for consumption by the public. A small Bed and Breakfast establishment has obviously to comply with the same regulations as the largest Hilton Hotel. Among the most important requirements are: the premises must be clean and in good condition, with no risk of contamination during food handling or storage by dirt, germs, insects, mice, etc.; there must be adequate lighting, ventilation, washing and waste disposal facilities; those handling the food should wear suitable clean and washable protective clothing, and if unwell, should report infectious illnesses to prevent their spread via the food being handled; and in order to prevent the growth of food-poisoning bacteria, one should maintain a minimum temperature for hot foods and a maximum temperature for cold foods. You may have to provide refrigeration.

Often the only way the Environmental Health Officer (the

person responsible for enforcing the regulations) finds out about a new Bed and Breakfast business is when a guest complains about mouldy food, filthy toilets or falling ill! Then the Environmental Health Officer will usually visit unannounced, to see whether the owner has been complying with the regulations. It has been known for them to find cigarette ends in the fridge, dirty washing piled high in the kitchen, greasy walls and a filthy cooker.

Even if sure your home will never be like that, they would prefer you to go along and ask their advice before any guests arrive. Such advice will usually take the form of a visit to see how the regulations may affect your particular premises. It is unlikely, provided that they are clean, in good condition and that you yourself aim for a high standard of hygiene, that many changes will have to be made. Possibly, if doing Bed and Breakfast, the only necessary changes will be to install an extra basin in the kitchen for hand-washing, or arrange for dustbins to be stored well away from food.

Animals and birds should never be allowed in the kitchen during the day or to sleep. So train pets, before any guests come, to get used to sleeping in another part of the house.

In the country, where there is a septic tank or a private water supply, the Environmental Health Officer will also ensure that the tank is large enough to cope with additional waste, and test a sample of water to see that it is free from contamination. If it were not, they would correct it.

If you are hoping to serve your own 'untreated' milk to visitors, the local Environmental Health Officer or nearest Ministry of Agriculture Office will advise you, as there are additional regulations to be complied with.

Although it can all sound rather daunting, the continual aim must be a high standard of hygiene. Guests are unlikely to return if you are careless about the Hygiene Regulations. Do not forget, too, to look presentable the day the Environmental Health Officer comes to visit and not as if you have just dug the garden or fed the pigs. It will help enormously if you look as clean and tidy as the kitchen and the rest of the house are supposed to be!

Insurance

If a Fire Certificate is not required, a normal home insurance policy may be valid. However, an additional premium will have to be paid to extend the public liability cover which is necessary by law. This insures guests, any employees and the public from accidental injury or damage arising in connection with the business. It also covers loss or damage to guests' property, though not loss of your own valuables or property due to theft by a guest, as this type of policy only covers theft by forcible entry or exit. The insurance agent will usually ask for a signed assurance that not more than six guests will be accommodated.

If more than six guests are staying, a business policy for hotels and guest houses will be required. The agent will need to see the Fire Certificate and will have to know the maximum number of guests staying at any one time. The same policy covers guest houses with three rooms and hotels with a hundred rooms. Only the premiums differ. If the business is seasonal, for example closed in winter, it is usually possible to pay a reduced premium.

Even if less than six guests are planned, this type of policy is to be recommended if people come regularly, as the insurance cover will be much greater. You will be insured for employers' and public liability, damage to stock and other contents by theft (not necessarily by forcible entry), storm, flood, fire, etc. The insurance man, as well as the Fire Prevention Officer, will want to see a well-cared-for kitchen and fire extinguishers handy. With a business policy you are also covered for loss of income should the guest house need to be closed because of flood, fire, explosion, etc. In this event it is important to estimate correctly the time it may take to re-open for business, and the profits which may be lost. There is no point in insuring for only twelve months if the structural work after a fire, for example, would keep the house shut for longer. Then, if the worst occurs, at least the insurance would be adequate.

Cover is usually extended against loss of money both on the business premises as well as from a bank night-safe or in transit; personal injury as a result of a hold-up or criminal assault is also included. Optional cover can be given too for food accidentally damaged in the freezer, damage to signs, office equipment, etc.

Breakages, however, are likely to be covered only under a more expensive 'all risks' policy. So the important thing is to keep such valuables as vases and glass away from guests!

If you ask anyone taking in paying guests the one thing they are most afraid of, the answer is likely to be 'poisoning the guests accidentally'! It is bad enough when the family has to retire to bed with severe tummy-ache, but when guests do likewise, it is not very good for business. The public liability section of the insurance policy covers you against such an eventuality, but do make sure that the financial protection it gives is adequate. The snowball effect when one landlady's guest was stricken with food poisoning is worth remembering. He missed his train as a result of frequent stops on the way; being self-employed and absent from his business for a week, he suffered loss of earnings. He claimed in court against the guest-house owner for his extreme discomfort, loss of earnings, solicitors' fees and so on! Even defending oneself, a case like this can prove costly, and will only be met by the company if insurance is adequate. As always, with any kind of insurance, check the policy regularly to ensure that present cover is still adequate, especially if the business has grown. And *never* under-insure. This is another way of saying never underestimate the guests! A common claim against insurance from guest houses and hotels is for furniture damaged by cigarette burns. If you do not think that a few guests could be so unthoughtful and stub their cigarettes out on the furniture, ask the insurance man. He will tell you otherwise!

Employing Additional Staff

Although you may start in a very small way, there could soon come a time when you would like someone to help, even on a part-time basis—usually because you are expanding and can take in more guests. Having another person to help enables you to stop to talk to a guest, knowing someone is on hand to continue the work. It is no good burning the toast because you are too busy greeting the visitors in the morning!

But no matter how prettily the table is decorated, or how good the cooking, inferior service will spoil any effect you may be hoping to achieve. If someone else will be waiting on the guests, or greeting them at the door, it is essential that they are neat, tidy and presentable. It will add greatly both to your peace of mind and to the enjoyment and appreciation of the guests if you have someone working for you who is reliable and will make as much effort as you do when meeting guests.

However, employing someone, whether casually or full-time, means complying with the various Acts of Parliament drawn up for the employee's protection. Insurance must be provided lest the person employed should suffer injury while at work. You should give them written details of the main terms of employment, pay them at least minimum wage rates and deduct tax and National Insurance contributions where necessary. To find out more about an employer's obligations, there are booklets and advice available from the local Department of Employment.

One is also responsible, under the Health and Safety at Work Act, for ensuring the health, safety and welfare at work of anyone employed by you. *Which?* magazine found in a survey they conducted that many people seriously underestimated health and safety hazards at home. Among other things, they found too little use of anti-slip flooring, electrical appliances not regularly serviced, no fire extinguishers or fire blankets and inadequate first-aid kits. So make your kitchen and the rest of the home a safe place, not only for guests, but for anyone working in it.

Trade Descriptions Act and Price Display

Not only is it very important to be fair and honest about your house with guests, there is also a legal requirement to do so. When describing your house and the availability of facilities and services provided, any statements, both verbal and written, must be accurate and not misleading in any way. Statements in the advertising and brochures must also be true. If there is an illustration of the property, it must not give a false impression. If telling a prospective guest that it is only a mile to the nearest shops, or the sea, it would be reasonable of them to expect to cover that mile on foot or in a car. You would be misleading them if it was one mile as the crow flies, but five by road!

If offering sleeping accommodation of at least eight beds or four bedrooms, it is necessary to display overnight charges prominently.

The Trading Standards or Consumer Protection Officer is able to give more advice on this, as well as on the Trades Descriptions Act and how that may apply to your business. He will also be able to advise you on the display of charges if considering serving lunches or dinners to non-resident guests.

Licensing Laws and Value Added Tax

A solicitor will advise on the correct procedures should you wish to sell alcoholic drink to resident guests in your home, as it will be necessary to apply for a licence. He will apply on your behalf to the Licensing Justices (in England and Wales) at the Magistrates' Court for a residential licence, enabling you to sell alcoholic drink to residents and their friends for consumption on the premises. You will also need to keep a register of resident guests which the police can inspect at any time. Once a licence has been granted, you have obligations under the Weights and Measures Act to supply standard measures of alcoholic drink.

Although the service itself which is provided by those who take in paying guests is taxable at the standard rate of Value Added Tax, it is unlikely, if guests come on a small scale, that your turnover would reach the taxable limit. (In 1981 the tax threshold stood at £15,000; consult your local Customs and Excise office for the current limit.) Registration for VAT will in most cases not be beneficial. The bulk of any expenditure is on food, which is zero-rated, and you would only be able to claim back a small amount on other items, for example toilet rolls and kitchen equipment. It would also raise prices, as guests would have to be charged VAT on their bill, quite likely to lead to a reduction in their numbers!

If, however, you fall into one of the following categories, or have any doubts about registering, you will need specialised advice from the local Customs and Excise office. Providing Bed and Breakfast on the scale of a small hotel will possibly mean your taxable turnover could exceed the current limits set. Estimate the possible turnover for the next twelve months, i.e. all the money which you could receive from guests without any expenses deducted, and if you believe you may exceed the taxable limit, you should notify Customs and Excise of your liability to be registered.

Second, one has to bear in mind, with VAT, that it is the person and not the business who is registered, so if you have other taxable business activities which until now have not reached the VAT limit, running an additional Bed and Breakfast business may suddenly make you liable for this tax.

Last, if thinking of running Bed and Breakfast from a farmhouse, it is advisable to consult one's accountant or the local Customs and Excise office. Because all the taxable business activities of a person are combined, taking in paying guests is considered to be an accountable activity of the farmer, despite the fact that most of the work is usually done by his wife and the rest of the family! The Bed and Breakfast side of the farm must be seen to be run independently of the rest of the farm business before the wife is considered separately for VAT.

3

Finance, Advertising and Bookings

Initial Finance

It is unlikely that anyone at the beginning of their Bed and Breakfast business will have all the furniture and fittings needed. There may not be sufficient crockery, sheets, tables, etc. Alterations may have to be made to the house to give more space, or to comply with Fire Regulations. Car parking space may be required. And in order to attract the guests there is the advertising to consider. If one has no money available for these items, the bank manager is the first person to approach for his advice on possible sources of finance.

But it is no good going along just on the off-chance that he will agree to an overdraft or loan without knowing anything about your plans. It will be necessary to present your case for additional finance to him in a way which will make him see the potential and future success of the project! You yourself have to be convinced it will work. You then have to convince the bank manager and he may have to convince someone in higher authority if you are asking for a large amount of money. So one must be prepared for all the questions he is bound to ask. Even if you only plan to take in one or two guests occasionally, the bank manager will still see it in terms of a small 'business'.

He will require a 'forecast' of the expected income and expenditure. This means that you must have a good idea how many guests can be accommodated, how much each guest will be charged, and the total income over the Bed and Breakfast period. He will also want to know the expenditure on such items as food, repairs, renewals, rates, electricity and other services, insurance and day-to-day running costs. What is left after those costs have been deducted will be your 'income', out of which will come the loan repayments. That is why it is very important to have all the possible running costs worked out before going to see him. He will also want details of any experience you may have for beginning this kind of business. From this he will be able to assess whether it is likely to be viable. Is there anyone who will help out if you are ill? The house may be full of guests, but if you are not well, he has to be sure that the business will continue.

All this information is more important if the business is several years old and the reason for going to see him is for a possible loan for expansion. Although he is already likely to know the state of your finances, he will want to have a current evaluation of progress. This will help him assess your borrowing needs. If your proposals are sound and carefully presented, you stand a much greater chance of obtaining the extra finance.

If the bank is unable to help, or can only contribute some of the capital and the Bed and Breakfast business is sited in a development or intermediate development area, it may be possible to obtain financial assistance from the Tourist Board. They give discretionary grants or loans towards the capital costs of setting up or improving a tourist project. This would include running a small guest house, providing accommodation for tourists. For details of the eligible areas and the scheme itself, apply to your regional Tourist Board. But remember that, similar to other forms of grant aid, it is necessary to apply before any work on the project has started.

The Council for Small Industries in Rural Areas (COSIRA) also makes loans towards the provision of additional accommodation and improvement of existing accommodation in Bed and Breakfast establishments, farmhouses and small guest houses. This only applies to rural areas, small towns and special development areas. Details of the areas concerned and the loans can be obtained from your local COSIRA office.

The regional Tourist Board for your particular area may also be able to give advice on any other likely sources of financial help.

Prices

Deciding how much guests will pay is a difficult thing to do when first starting. You obviously want to keep within the range of other charges in the area: in that way everyone is fair to each other. Also, if charges are much less than other local Bed and Breakfast houses, prospective guests will be suspicious about the service you provide! If they are too high, they may consider it more reasonable to go elsewhere. The best way to inquire about local rates is to ask or phone similar sized houses to your own and find out how much they charge. But bear in mind that they may offer a different service to the one that you hope to provide. They may give an evening meal, have wash-basins in all the rooms, etc. A few inquiries will soon determine what they are providing for the money. Once you are established and you know similar landlords or landladies, it will soon become apparent that they often compare their prices openly with others in the business. In this way they get a guide to how reasonable they themselves are being.

Because prices obviously have to be worked out in advance of the first guests' arrival, one has also to bear in mind possible rises in the cost of food, electricity, rates, etc. which may occur throughout the coming season. A sudden surcharge on a bill in the middle of August just after the electricity bill has arrived will not be very welcome!

Your running costs to be considered include food, advertising and postage, repairs, maintenance of equipment and facilities, wear and tear on crockery, sheets, furniture, etc., insurance, electricity and telephone charges, casual labour costs and so on. The amount you charge must cover all these expenses and give you a profit margin on top. Remember too that there are likely to be times when you have fewer visitors but some running costs remain constant (e.g. insurance and rates).

It is usual to add on approximately 10 per cent to your prices for those guests staying less than four nights, which covers such additional costs as laundry. And from the guests' point of view, do ensure that any daily or weekly charges are inclusive of things like constant hot water and laundry facilities. Long-term travellers in particular appreciate the need for regular bathing and washing of clothes. Asking for extra payment for a bath, for example, is seen by many tourists to be petty and mean. Most would prefer to pay a higher tariff and have such things as bathing included in the price.

It is obviously going to be much more difficult in the first year of business to estimate all one's expenses. However, do not start too cheaply, thinking you can put prices up next year to recoup some of the previous expenses. It will only make people suspicious when they discover next year's prices have risen dramatically. Similarly, after a year or two, if prices have been kept down for too long, it is not a good idea suddenly to increase them by too great a percentage the following season. Keep to slow gradual price rises. Don't be afraid, however, to do a bit of 'marketing' in your business and perhaps have special offers of accommodation. Reduced rates in spring and autumn for two- or three-day 'breathers' or 'children under five free' will often bring in business during a quieter year. It always makes more sense to keep the house as fully occupied as possible. You'll probably put in as much work for two guests as for half a dozen with a much smaller return!

It is unreasonable to expect that doing Bed and Breakfast will bring you vast amounts of money very quickly! Some say that in the first year, expect to make a loss. This may especially be true when you have spent a considerable amount of money on basic items of furniture and equipment; there is greater outlay when setting up the business. Also, in the first year you are not going to be as full as you would like. It will take a while to feel your way and build up a regular turnover. The second year you may break even and only in the third will you make any profit. Obviously one has to take a long-term view and it will be a few years before one can properly assess progress, but do always allow yourself a fair profit margin (at least two-fifths). If the profit margin is too small, you will find that you are working too hard for too little return. Guests tend to believe they are getting what they are paying for. If a high standard is the aim, a fair price must be charged. Only undercut if it is not going to mean an appreciable loss of quality.

Day-to-day Finance

If you begin by taking a small number of guests, it will be possible to keep your own accounts. To help keep track of running costs, have a weekly budget especially for food, and make a note of the day-to-day expenses in a cashbook. Write everything down, phone calls, postage, cost of food, etc. (including a realistic assessment of the mileage covered to buy it). By spending one evening a week checking over the figures it should be easy to ensure that one has not overspent. The first year in business is obviously the most expensive in terms of equipment. Receipts for all the large purchases will be needed when ascertaining which expenses may be tax-deductible.

As the business grows, the services of an accountant may be advisable if you are unable to cope with these things yourself. (Remember that all the finances have to be dealt with in an already busy week.) The local Citizens' Advice Bureau will arrange an appointment with an accountant if you do not already have one. Every bill and invoice must be safely kept. You will need copies of everything, one for yourself, another for the accountant. These copies and also a well maintained account or cashbook are also vital for income tax purposes at the end of the financial year.

Advertising

Once you have decided on the prices to be charged, the prospective visitor now has to be told that you are open for business and that there are advantages in coming to you, as opposed to the Bed and Breakfast place along the road! After the first year or so, many of your guests are hopefully going to become regulars, or will at least give their friends a personal recommendation, and you may then be able to cut down a little on the advertising. But in the beginning you have to do all you can to attract your first visitors.

There is a very delicate balance between having sufficient advertising to bring in guests but not overspending. A method of monitoring the adverts in the first few years will give you a good indication which ones are most productive. Either add a letter or number (indicating to you a specific publication) in your return address, for example after your name, or, if answering a phone

inquiry, simply ask the person where they saw the advertisement. You will then be able to confine further advertising to the most effective publications.

Although it is usual to begin advertising as soon as possible after Christmas, as planning a summer holiday seems to cheer most people up in the long winter months, one must be careful to retain some finance for later, more last-minute adverts. Many holidaymakers are not planning ahead quite so much as they used to, and you may well find that it is not until May or June that they are happy to book their holiday.

Newspapers and Periodicals

These can be expensive forms of publicity, but you may consider it worth it in terms of the large readership figures involved. For many already in business this is their only method of advertising. The most effective way is to place an advert in a national daily or Sunday paper of your choice once a week for six weeks, beginning mid-January until the end of February. The dailies often have one particular day when the holiday ads go in, and may have special terms, for example six weeks for the price of five, available. Then continue with an advert in a monthly magazine in March and April. In that way there will always be an advert for your accommodation appearing regularly during the winter months. If you have no particular preference about the paper used, your local newsagent will be able to give advice. A monthly magazine which caters for facilities to be found in your particular area is a wise choice. It may pertain to yachting or trout fishing. Or it could cater for a special type of reader, such as retired people or church-goers, who may be especially welcome as your guests.

Convey in the advertisement some of the most important features of the house and service provided. Is it in the country or by the sea? Are children and pets welcome? Do you give an evening meal? Also, give an indication of the price charged. Familiarising yourself with the abbreviations to be used in the ad —H and C, W.C., E.M. etc.—will enable you to make the most effective use of the space. If telephoning the advert in to the paper concerned, the sales people are usually very helpful at guiding the novice through all the appropriate terminology!

Guidebooks

There are many guidebooks available from newsagents and bookshops which list Bed and Breakfast establishments throughout the United Kingdom. Some of the most useful of these are listed in Appendix B. There are regional guides, farm holiday guides, those produced by motoring organisations and so on. Prices of advertising vary considerably. One of their principal disadvantages for the beginner is the fact that they are often produced more than a year ahead, so they are a more practical proposition for your second and succeeding years. They very often include a sketch or photograph of the house as well as details about accommodation.

You can mention much more information in a guidebook about yourself than is possible in a newspaper advertisement. Among other things, state whether open all year round, or just in the summer. If you have decided to stay open during the winter months, supply low-season rates (usually 5–10 per cent lower than summer ones). Mention a Fire Certificate if you have one, any facilities for disabled guests, and give an indication of whether a car would be advisable, or if there is public transport nearby. Do you provide a typical British breakfast and good home cooking? If your home is a farm, are pets welcome, and can guests help with farm life? By emphasising aspects of the accommodation you feel to be particularly attractive, you are most likely then to appeal to like-minded guests.

Tourist Boards

It is possible to register with both the National and the regional Tourist Board and become listed in their accommodation guides. For details, contact the Tourist Board covering your particular area. Although this is one of the most useful ways to advertise, it is again not always possible in the first year of business, as the guides tend also to be prepared in advance.

When placing an advertisement in any of the guides which are prepared months ahead, do be especially careful that your estimation of running costs, and thus your prices for the next year, are accurate. You may have to work them out in February of one year for publication, anticipating possible expenses through until October or November of the next.

Local Information Offices and Tourist Guides

Apart from those guests booking their holiday in advance through newspapers, guides, etc., the touring holidaymakers also make up a large percentage of Bed and Breakfast visitors. They do not in fact want to plan their route or overnight stops too much in advance. One of the needs they have when they arrive in a new area is to find reliable accommodation. So registration with the local tourist information office will ensure a good chance of such visitors coming your way.

Without help from a tourist information centre, a tourer may miss you altogether if you are off the beaten track, preferring instead to stay on the main road. If in such an isolated position, provide the office with maps giving directions to your house. For anyone unfamiliar with the area, one country lane can look much like another!

Many local information offices also keep a central list of vacancies which is updated every day. Go in regularly to see them. These personal visits help to establish contact between yourself and the staff, often volunteers, who man them. They may often be able to recommend you personally to prospective visitors, and by ringing in every morning about any spare rooms, you are likely to attract spur of the moment guests.

There are annual publications, too, produced by towns or holiday areas, in which you can advertise. A lot of tourers use these and will give you a ring earlier in the day, before making their way to the area, knowing that they have somewhere to stay.

Other Publicity

Once the season is under way, one can, quite cheaply, use many other ways of advertising. Cards will go in shop windows, a very effective way of attracting passing guests. The local post office, police station and garages should also be told that you now take paying guests. For strangers, these are obvious ports of call to inquire about accommodation, especially in country areas. And tell them too about any vacancies as they arise, so that they can be kept up to date. Lastly, do not be afraid to tell other guest houses that you have opened. There will always be a proportion of visitors who turn up every year because the house down the road was full and they have been sent to you instead! Hopefully there will come a day when you are fully booked and can return the favour.

Signs

These are the most useful indications to those on a motoring holiday that you provide accommodation. However, there are regulations affecting the size and situation of the sign used, and the local Planning Office should be consulted. Provided the size of the sign is within certain limits and is erected within the boundary of the property concerned, there is usually no problem. The situations they like to avoid are the ones in which your establishment is advertised from a long way away with signs at every few yards! In conservation areas and national parks there are usually different regulations which you will need to inquire about.

Any sign used does need to be professional looking, reflecting the care and concern taken inside the home. A badly made, tatty sign may give the impression that the house is similarly shoddy!

Many houses display a Vacancies/No Vacancies notice on their sign. This is an advantage for the prospective guests, as they can see immediately whether rooms are available. For you as the owner there is a major drawback. When someone to whom you take an instant dislike comes to the door, it is a lot more difficult to think of excuses why you do not want them to stay if your sign is proudly proclaiming vacancies! It does happen from time to time, and you may prefer to retain the option of turning away these callers.

Brochures

After inquiries have come in from advertisements in newspapers, etc. (and you should at least get a few!) it is useful to have a brochure to send back. It saves you at this stage having to write a long descriptive letter. Prospective guests can read the brochure at their leisure, possibly compare it with others, and decide if yours is the kind of place they would like.

It need not be too elaborate, as you must always avoid unnecessary expense. Find a good, cheap printer to produce it, and have sufficient done at one time to last two or three years, by leaving space to insert prices. This avoids increased printing costs. There could be a sketch or photograph of the house on the front, and a map on the back to enable guests to find you without too much trouble. Include details and times of meals, car parking, information about children and pets etc. and a general description of the area. It is always much better to under-elaborate in the brochure, and then no one will be too disappointed! And you have obligations under the Trades Descriptions Act. Always tell the truth about the area. If it is on top of a hill and very windy, it is better that prospective visitors know. Then you will not get those who hate to be blown about, and will complain all day to you. Similarly, if living miles from the nearest shop or pub, you are more likely to attract those who want to get away from it all. Fairness to the guests is most important.

You can also include in the brochure details and approximate cost of any transport arrangements you may consider making for guests who will arrive on their own two feet. In case they come laden with sufficient clothes to cater for every change in the British weather, they may appreciate transport arranged for them from the nearest coach or train station. Nothing is more tiring than having to walk a long distance in a strange town after an uncomfortable journey, carrying the holiday clothes and with two or three children in tow! In the country there will obviously be a much longer drive to meet guests with no car. If no one in the family will have sufficient time to do this (and it will no doubt be a busy Saturday) you could arrange for a local taxi or mini-cab service instead.

If your facilities will enable you to take disabled guests, it is most important to ensure that any details about them are accurate. It is much more helpful to include measurements of rooms, doorways and so on than to provide simply a general description. Anyone with facilities for disabled guests can also let Holiday Care Service (address in Appendix B) know. They hold details of suitable accommodation not only for people who are disabled, but also the elderly or those with special family circumstances, for example those looking for budget holidays, or holidays suitable for single parents or unaccompanied children.

As business expands, you may feel that the cost of printed notepaper, cards, postcards and even ceramic tiles with a photo or sketch of your house is justified. These prove to be very popular and practical souvenirs for guests when returning home.

Bookings

Before your first bookings come in, it is vital to buy a large diary with plenty of space for each day's entries. Keep it by the telephone and write each name in as you take the booking. Have all your rooms numbered, at least in your head, and mark the number of each room against each name. It has been known, especially among those just starting, to double-book a room!

Once an inquiry has been received, a suggested reply would go something like this:

> Thank you very much for your inquiry received this morning. At the time of writing, we are pleased to be able to offer you accommodation for the dates required. Our aim is to provide you, our guests, with plenty of good food, fresh air and a relaxed atmosphere in which you can unwind.

You can include something here about the town, beach or farm etc., depending on what you feel you are offering. Then answer any queries they have put in their letter about pets or linen, etc. 'I enclose a brochure for your guidance. The terms are shown.'

State too if you would like a deposit (usually 10 per cent). This 10 per cent deposit at the time of booking usually ensures a firm reservation. The deposit is returnable in the event of cancellation, providing the accommodation is re-let for the period booked. Deposit money can also be used as the season progresses to finance late advertising. Mention the time you would like them to vacate the bedroom on the last day: 'We trust that we may have the pleasure of a visit from you, and we assure you of our best service at all times. Yours sincerely . . .'

Once a definite offer of accommodation, either verbal or in writing, is made by you, and it has been unconditionally accepted by the guest within a reasonable time, a valid and binding contract exists. From that time you are obliged to keep the accommodation available for the guests and they are obliged to take up and pay for it. If a prospective guest phones to book, it is a good idea to ask him to confirm it in writing as soon as possible, as you then have a record of the rooms he requires. Also ask him, if not previously mentioned, for the number of people in the party, the ages of the children, if any, the type of rooms required (single or double), and for details of any special requirements such as cots, high chairs, special diets or facilities.

Your attention to their particular needs at this preliminary stage is an important contribution to the success of the holiday.

4

Guest Rooms

There is often a moment of panic when you realise that the guests will very soon be arriving to live in your house. Until this time, you probably did not think of them as 'real' people at all!

What are they actually going to need in their bedrooms? How can you make the dining-room as attractive as possible? What will you say to them?

As one of the most common reasons for starting Bed and Breakfast is the need for extra cash, it is possible that you will not be able to make as many changes to the house as you would like in the first year.

Any initial cash is likely to have been swallowed up in brochures and advertising costs, and it makes good sense not to rush out on a spending spree for furniture and equipment until the first guests have booked and the business is seen to have potential. Many people have started with very little, and local auction rooms and sales will provide furniture which is likely to last for many years. Improving facilities is a gradual process. At the end of each year you add more.

It is, however, advisable to buy the best quality you can afford at the time. To have to replace cheap and shoddy goods every few years only depletes any capital you may be trying to build up.

Disabled Guests

The bedrooms for guests' use are likely to be up one or two flights of stairs. However, if there is a downstairs room easily convertible into a bedroom, this could be equipped for a wheelchair user and people with limited walking ability. Many disabled people and many families with disabled children are not able to have a holiday because small guest houses often do not provide access and facilities. The English Tourist Board Requirements for the Physically Handicapped are in Appendix A. And there is also available free from the English Tourist Board an advisory handbook on *Providing for Disabled Visitors.* This gives more advice on catering for physically handicapped guests. Even if few structural changes are planned, the addition of such things as ramps and handrails can mean a welcome to guests who are not wholly confined to a wheelchair, and can walk for short distances.

The Bedroom

In Appendix A the minimum standards of the English Tourist Board for serviced accommodation are given, a useful guide to the basic requirements.

The beds are obviously the most important items, the number of beds in each room depending on its size. If it is a large room, a double and two singles enable you to take a small family. The space is better utilised with four people sleeping there rather than two. In a smaller room, two singles are more versatile than a double, and they can always be pushed together should a double be needed. It is now possible to buy single beds which zip together, and this could be a future purchase. Choose beds that are durable, comfortable and adaptable. They should be clean (very important if buying second-hand beds from auctions or sales), well sprung, and firm rather than soft. It is a good idea if you and other members of the family can spend a night or two on each one before the visitors come. If it is difficult to have a good night's sleep on them, the guests are very likely to feel the same way! Nothing ruins a holiday more than sleeping on an uncomfortable mattress, and you do not really want to be greeted every morning by guests with weary faces, clutching their aching backs!

Bunk beds are ideal for older children. As top bunks should not be used by those under five, even with a safety rail, convert them back into two singles when younger families stay.

Life will be very much easier for families with a baby if a high chair and a cot can be supplied on request. But the old cot in the attic must be thoroughly checked before use. Among other things, it should have high sides and edges, and no horizontal bars or ledges to help the baby to climb out. There should be no sharp edges to get cut on and no dangerous gaps to fall through. It should also be painted with non-toxic lead-free paint. If buying a new cot for guests' use, make sure it is marked with a kitemark or British Standards number.

The mattresses need cotton covers which can be cleaned easily. If the bed is likely to be used by young children put a rubber sheet on top of the mattress cover. Although most parents tell you when their child is likely to wet the bed, it is far better to have to wash just a sheet and blanket than have a damp, stained mattress. It helps to put another blanket between the mattress and the bottom sheet, as it provides added warmth and comfort, yet it is often missing in many guest-house beds.

Although Continental quilts are the usual form of bedding in guest houses in many parts of Europe, the British weather makes airing of these large and bulky items difficult. You are unlikely to be able to hang them out of the windows for very long in the morning before the rain comes! So the most satisfactory way of making up the bed is still with good old-fashioned sheets and blankets.

Nylon and terylene sheets are easy to wash and dry, but are not so efficient at absorbing the body's moisture. Cotton or a polyester and cotton mix are preferable. They wash well, need little ironing, and have the tremendous advantage of being able to be sent to the laundry, coming back ready for immediate use.

If using coloured sheets, the co-ordination of the colour scheme in the bedroom is important. However much you like black sheets and red walls, the guests may not!

Provide plenty of blankets and leave several in the room for guests to add if cold at night. Two pillows each will cater for most visitors, as there are usually very individual preferences. But none should be supplied with a cot.

The bedrooms will have blinds, or curtains, and if likely to be used by children, it is well worth while lining the curtains well.

Parents, especially on holiday, appreciate their children sleeping as late as possible. An early wakening, due to the sun shining through thin curtains, is not usually welcome!

Fitted carpets or carpets tacked to the floor make the room easier to clean, with no wooden surrounds to gather dust. They are also safer than rugs or mats. If rugs are used, they should have an anti-slip base.

You can never have enough hangers in the wardrobe! If in doubt about how much space each guest may need in drawers and wardrobes, err on the side of plenty. Assume they are going to bring everything with them, including the kitchen sink!

If windows do not look too safe for children in family rooms, and it could be easy for them to fall out, fit lockable catches or bolts.

Central heating may well be an improvement lined up for the future. If you do not have it at the moment, and are hoping to have visitors out of season, some form of heater in the bedrooms will be essential. Shop around and look for the most practical, economical bedroom heater. Again, safety is the most important consideration. Guests may include the elderly, or they may be inquisitive toddlers reaching out to touch everything they can. Do not use a heater which can be knocked over, which will ignite bedding if put too close or which can set a passing dressing-gown or night-dress alight. The heater, in normal everyday use, must be safe.

Eventually each bedroom should have a wash-basin with hot and cold running water. This may not be possible in the first year, but it should be an early improvement. Most visitors now want Hot and Cold in their bedrooms, and this is one aspect of doing Bed and Breakfast where, if you do not keep up with the Joneses, guests will not come to you, but go down the road in preference! A wash-basin in the rooms also puts a lot less strain on the bathroom, and enables guests to wash any small items of clothes. Second-hand basins can often be picked up cheaply from sales or local builders' merchants. But the installation should first be checked with the council offices concerned with building regulations to ensure satisfactory drainage etc.

Razor points, mirrors, a waste-paper bin and bedside lights are other bedroom essentials. A box of tissues, a vase of freshly cut flowers or a pot plant will also add a few homely touches to the room. If commercial travellers are among your regular visitors, they may appreciate a clock radio to wake them in the mornings.

It is becoming increasingly popular to provide tea- or coffee-making facilities in the bedrooms. This spares the breakfast cook, probably you, from another job at the busiest time of day. A tea-making machine can be put in each bedroom, or simply an electric kettle, teapot, cups, tea, milk, sugar, etc., renewed each day. Apart from providing early morning tea or a bedtime drink, guests fill up flasks, or just pop back for a cuppa after a long walk in the country, a day's sightseeing or a swim in the sea.

As it is not something most tourists carry in their suitcases, shoe-cleaning equipment could be very welcome. Fill a large ice-cream carton with two brushes, a duster and both black and brown polish. Mark it and store it in the bottom of the wardrobe.

For smoking guests leave plenty of ashtrays around the room. This will greatly reduce any fire risk in bedrooms, as smokers will continue to smoke whether ashtrays are provided or not. It is possible to approach breweries or pubs for ashtrays which carry their advertising. They are often very willing to give them away.

In each bedroom, a small notice giving the times of the meals can also be displayed. This saves guests from continually asking. Many will simply forget.

Stairs and Landing

The Home Accident Surveillance System, which is operated by the Consumer Safety Unit of the Department of Trade, monitors accidents which occur in the home by collecting details from accident victims in twenty hospitals in England and Wales; they find that stairs and steps are one of the features of the home most frequently involved in accidents. So one must ensure that any carpets in these areas are in good repair and firmly fixed. Banisters must be secure too, and close enough together to stop children falling through. The landing and stair lights have to be left on in the evening and throughout the night. It is only common sense, but can take a little while to adjust to the idea if you, as a family, have become accustomed to switching them off whenever you go to bed. Obviously such running costs have to be taken into account when working out your charges.

Bathroom and Toilet

It will soon become apparent, within a short time of taking paying guests, that you can never have enough bathrooms and toilets! If starting Bed and Breakfast in a small way, it is probable that there is only one bathroom and toilet in the house. If someone in the family likes half an hour to themselves in the bathroom, he is not likely to get it at any time he wants once there are paying guests who need access to the bathroom at all reasonable times. Between seven and nine in the morning, as well as guests using the bathroom, there may be one's own children getting ready for school and a spouse preparing for work. Wash-hand basins certainly ease the congestion, but having an extra toilet avoids queues and frustration, and saves resentment building up between one's family and the guests. If planning to purpose-build a bathroom and toilet, or make structural changes to accommodate guests, have the bathroom and toilet separate. You could put a small shower unit in the bedrooms too if there is sufficient space. This reduces the amount of water used and the time spent (by the guest) in the bathroom. Although it does mean more cleaning in the bedrooms, more than the usual rate can be charged.

The bathroom needs clean towels and soap as required, a disposal bin for guests' use, and a good supply of toilet paper in the loo. Never let a guest be caught without at a crucial moment! In the country where there may be septic tank drainage, guests from town may not be familiar with the fact that what goes in either liquefies or has to come out again! For that reason, a tactful notice will be needed explaining that no cardboard, cotton wool, disposable nappies etc. should be put down the toilet. Disposal bins and bags should be provided and the contents incinerated daily.

Constant hot water in bedrooms and bathrooms can be expensive. Install the cheapest form of water heating. There are plenty of brochures available showing the various heating appliances (gas, electric or solid fuel), and further advice is easily obtainable. A separate bathroom heater should be permanently wired in, be high on the wall and should have a pull-cord on/off switch. Floor surfaces and mats in the bathroom should be non-slip.

Dining-room

If there is enough space, the visitors' dining-room needs to be independent of your own eating area, unless mealtimes will not coincide. Both the guests and yourselves will be much more relaxed if away from each other when eating. If space is at a premium, have family meals in the kitchen, giving visitors the dining-room. There must be a living area which the family recognises as its own, and one door which you can crumple behind when you cannot stand the guests for a minute longer! They too are unlikely to return if they witness too much of Johnny fighting with Susan before school, or too many 'mornings after the night before'. Few families are without their disagreements, and running a Bed and Breakfast guest house can certainly add stress and strain. So it is advisable to provide yourself with space to air the family's feelings occasionally!

The guests' dining-room will be warm, attractively decorated and large enough to provide separate tables for each group of guests. Small tables seating four are best, as they can then be put together if you have a larger party. The guests then pass the time of day with each other, or keep themselves to themselves if they prefer. The mood of the whole week revolves round how one particular group of guests gets on with each other, and breakfast time certainly reflects that mood. Many guests take an instant dislike to each other and the atmosphere can sometimes be cut with a knife in the mornings! All guests have their own requirements for breakfast time. Some are chatty and lively, while others just want to be left to themselves to wake up. You have to be able to give them both a little of what they want.

Guests spend a lot of time in the dining-room, so you can come into your own with regard to its decoration, and reflect a lot of your own personality in it. On holiday, people like to see something a bit different, so ensure that the dining-room has a little bit of you on show. Put in something which no other dining-room has. If you can paint pictures, arrange flowers or collect cigarette cards, put them into the dining-room for the guests to share. They provide both a talking point and a guide to the kind of person you are. Guests need to know a little bit about you as well. They will want to trust and have confidence in the service you are providing. Putting a few personal touches round the room helps them to do this. If they do not like you, they will

not come back! Personal touches also highlight your other abilities, apart from the fact that you are a good cook.

If the house has oak beams and open fireplaces, highlight them. Hang copper and brass on the beams and light a fire at every opportunity. Guests from smokeless zones will gaze for hours into the embers, perfectly content. (But if it is likely that children or old people could ever be left alone in the room with an open fire, there is a legal requirement to make sure that it has an adequate fireguard.)

Use natural material such as wood or stone in a farmhouse or country cottage, but materials such as glass and plastic in a modern building, creating a more sophisticated atmosphere. Warm, subtle colours are easy on the eye. Make sure too that the colours of the curtains and carpets match the walls. Before the first guests come, view the room from every angle. See what they will see as they have their breakfast. Furniture has to be in the best position to create easy movement round the tables when serving. It is no good if you trip over a chair with the porridge! A light airy room is always easier to eat in. If the room tends to be dark, think about increasing the size of the windows at a later date. Meanwhile, by placing a few large mirrors round the room, more daylight will be reflected. Guests must be able to see what they are eating. But avoid fluorescent lighting, which is good in the kitchen for lighting awkward corners, but tends to make other rooms flat and uninteresting.

Ceilings are important, so if the room has a high one, put in a picture rail to make it appear lower. Or paint it darker for the same effect. Remove a picture rail and paint it in a light colour for the reverse effect.

You will reap rewards and compliments from guests on the way their meal is prepared if the table setting is attractive. In choosing whether to use a tablecloth or not remember they involve regular cleaning and often provide a temptation for small children to pull. A polished table-top, though, needs a good protective covering, or it will be ruined by hot dishes. When buying table mats, the cork, melamine, wood or rush-backed ones provide more protection. If you do like the idea of tablecloths but do not want the hassle of starching or laundry bills, invest in seersucker or non-iron varieties.

In the middle of each table there could be a simple dried or fresh flower arrangement. If kept small it will not block the guests' vision. Enormous bunches of flowers do have a tendency to inhibit conversation!

Allow sufficient space between each setting for elbows, and sufficient between the inner knives and forks for the plates. Work from the outside in order of use when laying knives and forks. If giving the choice of a fish dish, lay fish knives and forks with the others. Special cutlery, such as fruit spoons for grapefruit or melon, can be brought to the table with the dish.

There are many different ways of folding serviettes. The simplest and most effective ways at breakfast are either to fold and place on the side plate, or roll and put in napkin rings. Paper serviettes (bought in bulk) will cut down on the laundering necessary for linen napkins.

Sitting-room

If you decide to do Bed and Breakfast only, and the majority of guests stay for one or two nights, you can manage without a sitting-room. But when providing high tea or dinner, guests are likely to be with you most of the evening and need somewhere to go. Also on wet days they will appreciate being able to sit comfortably indoors. These are the times when they can get on your nerves! You take pity on them, make them endless cups of tea, and put your own plans further behind. If you have a lounge, put a television in it and keep a plentiful supply of books, games, playing cards and toys for any children. Have as many brochures, leaflets and maps available as possible. Most museums and places of interest are only too willing to give information on their activities. Display local pottery and other crafts so that guests can then go out to see them being made. Familiarise yourself with places of interest for children, and the local cinema times for wet days.

Guests, especially from overseas, like to talk to someone who knows the area, and they appreciate information on what is on and where to go.

Once they have got to know each other, and if you like them enough, you may consider entertaining them yourself once a week. It does not need to be every week (and there will be a few guests for whom you would not want to do it!), but perhaps when the weather is fine, the evening meal on a Friday could be a barbecue outdoors, or an informal buffet supper with wine. It is best to do this on a Friday before they go home on the Saturday. If you make too much effort when they have first come, they will not relax sufficiently. At the end of the week they should go away remembering their holiday happily.

5

Cleaning and
Essential Equipment

It is important to save energy by minimising the effort involved in regular cleaning. You will need it all elsewhere! Avoid uncarpeted floors if possible and simplify furniture in the rooms the guests use, so that you can vacuum round easily. The more ornaments on the sideboard, the more dusting needed, so keep the majority of them tucked away.

Any major house alterations and painting are usually done before the guests arrive each year, or at the quietest time of the year if you take guests all year round. Major spring-cleaning (such as cleaning carpets and curtains) could be done then too, using professional firms for the larger jobs. But the annual spring-cleaning need not be such a major operation if regular daily and weekly cleaning is done.

Daily Cleaning

One needs to hoover the areas used every day, especially the dining-room and the stairs, with a good vacuum cleaner. And keep them clear of small objects left lying around which people could trip over. Dust the dining-room (not forgetting to look upwards for cobwebs in lampshades and corners) and use polish where you can. The room always smells fresher. Ashtrays and waste-paper bins should be emptied and old newspapers cleared away.

In the bathroom, the sink will need a clean and the toilet, especially the seat, disinfected and polished. A toilet cleaner which can be left inside the bowl will help to maintain freshness. A solution of disinfectant and water can also be used to wipe round the floor or carpet nearest the toilet. (Store household cleaners and chemicals in a secure place well away from any children.)

Sinks in the guests' bedrooms should also be cleaned daily. If guests have not made their own beds, you can do so. After overnight guests, the sheets will need changing and the bedrooms hoovered and dusted in preparation for the next arrivals. If the guests were smokers, opening the windows, hoovering throughout and wiping round the skirtings and ledges with a cloth rinsed in a mild disinfectant solution will freshen the room. Every other day, hoover and dust the bedrooms.

In the kitchen, it will save an enormous amount of time every day if you are organised and tidy, and keep plates, cutlery, serviettes and all the items necessary for laying the tables conveniently together. (Trays or a trolley are useful for carrying them into the dining-room.) Tidy up and store breakfast cereals, sugar, salt and pepper together in the larder, with coffee and tea near the kettle with the teapots. If all these items are spread over the kitchen, you will find yourself walking miles in the morning and wonder why you feel worn out by lunch-time! Clean working surfaces, sinks, the cooker and floors every day.

Weekly Cleaning

For those with guests staying a week or two, change-over day is usually Saturday. This is the day when you are most likely to feel the strain, so try not to overdo it. It is better to pay out a few pounds to someone else on a Saturday morning to change beds and clean rooms, so that you can then welcome new guests and bid home-going ones goodbye in a relaxed manner. If there is only a little money available for casual labour, Saturday morning is the time to spend it.

The guests are not going to go home happy if they are ordered out of the bedrooms and pushed out of the door before they have finished packing, so that you can get on with the cleaning!

Change all longer-staying guests' sheets, pillow-cases and towels weekly. Although they will have been given ample towels to last a week, always be willing to give them fresh ones should they need them before the weekend. While in guests' bedrooms, wipe the skirtings and the rest of the paintwork with hot soapy water. Mirrors also need to be shining.

In the kitchen the fridge will require defrosting weekly and any stale food removed. Check too that there are sufficient supplies of the basic foodstuffs to see you well into the next week, and also that stocks of light bulbs, toilet rolls and soap are adequate.

At least once a month, clean the windows, employing a window cleaner for those you cannot reach. (A somewhat unorthodox but perfectly satisfactory way to clean windows is to wash them over with a solution of soapy water. Just as that is beginning to dry, wipe them thoroughly with a large piece of crumpled newspaper. They will then sparkle.) If not using stainless steel cutlery, polish EPNS silver-plated knives and forks with a proprietary cleaner. Teapots can also be done at the same time, paying particular attention to spouts and lids.

Equipment

To some extent this depends on the finances available and the number of guests being catered for. If only a few visitors are coming occasionally you may feel that you can manage with what you have already, and any additional money must be spent on those items which suit the household's priorities. Providing for large numbers of Bed and Breakfast guests, however, can be costly, so it is advisable to visit a wholesale cash and carry which sells catering equipment. Their prices will be competitive, and you will be able to buy large, practical items which will cope with the numbers you are catering for. If already in a tourist area, keep an eye open for hotel sales or auctions. One can often pick up job lots of teapots, crockery, etc. for very little outlay.

If the kitchen is small, with limited ventilation, an extractor fan or cooker hood can help to remove cooking smells and moisture. It would be well worth fitting one if making any structural alterations. The smell of breakfast cooking can easily spread to the rest of the house, and whereas about ten minutes before it is ready, a whiff of bacon frying may stimulate a guest's appetite, continual odours from the kitchen can be unpleasant. If you are one of those cooks, too, who makes a lot of clatter in the kitchen as you prepare, keep the door closed when working, and possibly increase soundproofing. Guests do not want to wake up to the sound of a brass band in the kitchen!

The existing domestic fridge will soon prove too small when taking paying guests. Remember that there will be a lot of milk, butter, bacon, eggs, etc. to store for guests as well as your own family's needs. The purchase of a large commercial-type fridge is the answer. They are so spacious that practically everything perishable will fit in. If living a long way from the shops, one is already likely to have a freezer. But if not, it would be well worth considering. The purchase of a freezer will enable you to do without the frozen food compartment in the fridge, giving more space for essential items. Both freezer and fridge need to be kept in a well ventilated area, and if the freezer can be kept in a colder outhouse or garage, it will be more economical to run.

Cooking breakfast for a large number of people on a battered old cooker can be very exhausting! If replacing your old cooker, make sure that the top is wide enough for three or four pans to sit at one time and give enough room for you to stir the contents comfortably. If hoping to do a lot of grilling, look for a cooker with a large grill. If you plan making your own bread regularly, a cooker with a large oven area or a fan oven may suit you best. And for the forgetful landlord or landlady, a microwave oven is a boon. Breakfast can come straight from the freezer into the microwave and on to the table in a very short time.

Toast is most conveniently made on a large catering-type toaster, which handles, automatically, at least six slices at a time. The larger the better as far as the toaster is concerned! With items such as this, which will be in use every day, always buy a size bigger than you think necessary at the time. Business will expand and you will be grateful when the dining-room is full of hungry people! And a two-gallon stainless steel urn will provide all the boiling water you need for tea and coffee without constantly having to refill kettles or pans. Saucepans, similarly, should be large enough to cope with guests' appetites, and heavy enough to be hard-wearing. Most guest-house owners would insist that at least two frying pans are essential. This enables eggs and, say, sausages to be cooked simultaneously. If you have not

already acquired most of the basic crockery, it is worth remembering that you are going to need teapots, water pots, jugs, sugar bowls, toast racks, egg cups, salt and peppers, sufficient cereal bowls, small fruit dishes, side plates and possibly fish knives and forks.

If the thought of having to wash all this up in the mornings fills you with dread, a dishwasher saves many tedious hours by the sink. It also keeps the kitchen much tidier as the dirty dishes are stored there until the washer is full. But it does mean that you need a larger number of dishes than you may otherwise require, and the ones you do have should be approved for use in the dishwasher.

It is also worth remembering, especially if guests will only be staying a night or two, that your own domestic washing machine may not cope. And even if it did, have you a tumble drier or sufficient space to dry countless sheets, towels etc.? The last thing guests want to see are sheets permanently drying in front of the fire or over radiators. It may be well worth your while to use the nearby launderette or a local laundry.

Naturally, individual preferences and practical considerations vary. Nevertheless, if you know people locally who have years of experience in taking paying guests then it is always worth asking them, informally, for their advice (and recommendations) on service, equipment, brand names and so on.

As with everything else, you will, in the end, decide for yourself what is going to suit you best. It is, after all, your home and your business.

6

Breakfast

Planning the Meal

If people feel that they are getting more than their value for money when they come and stay with you, they are bound to want to return or recommend your guest house to friends. As far as the food is concerned, aim for good quality from the outset. It is far better to charge slightly more and be generous with the food than to charge too little and find that all the way through the season you are forced to make economies. Visitors will know when you are trying to be mean with the food and naturally it is likely to make them feel very uncomfortable.

Give them the best food that their money will buy. If you are hoping to build up the business from year to year, you want the same guests to return. So you have to take a long-term view and provide quality in the catering. This does not mean, however, that you buy all your food in the most expensive shop in town. If you use a good cash and carry you can buy tea, coffee, butter, sugar, flour and all the other basic provisions in bulk. It will save money and ensure you are less likely to run short. Even fruit and vegetables can be bought in bulk from a wholesale greengrocer. Tomatoes, for instance, will be a lot cheaper that way, and fresh orange juice is certainly practical at times when you can pick up a crate of fresh oranges cheaply.

But do not neglect your local tradespeople. It helps enormously to develop good relations with them, especially the butcher and fishmonger. If you tell them that you are now taking paying guests they will advise you as to the best produce available. Show them that you want quality produce and they will be more than willing to help. Their advice is especially valuable with 'portion control'. It is no good just asking for four smoked haddock. They may all be different sizes, and out of four fish you may only have three portions. Your local fishmonger will soon learn what you need.

On the whole, however, you will need to have sufficient quantities of food for each day ahead. Check and if necessary restock on basic items such as eggs and bacon during the day. There is nothing worse than running out of eggs in the middle of breakfast. And do not forget to take other essential items out of the freezer the night before. Unless you possess a microwave oven, thawing a pack of frozen sausages at 8.45 in the morning is not easy!

If planning fish for breakfast the next morning, much of the essential preparation can be done in advance, so make a point of asking the previous evening which guests would like fish. This is probably the only time when it is helpful to know the guests' choice in advance.

Prepare as much as possible the evening before to help you cope with breakfast the next morning. Lay up the tables with cutlery and crockery, leaving only the last-minute items to put there in the morning before the guests come down. These will include plenty of sugar, cold milk, salt and pepper, butter or margarine, cereals and preserves. A variety of popular bottled sauces can be left on a side table in the dining-room should guests wish to use them. Many people now prefer polyunsaturated margarine to butter, and it is a good idea to have it available. If you treat the guests as individuals and find out their preferences, they will all feel as if they have your undivided attention. But do not get too carried away with trying to please all of them every time. There will usually be some guests who complain. One has to become accustomed to that. You must just be as under-standing and as reasonable as possible!

It is important to get up early enough to assess the needs of the next 24 hours. If you are well organised first thing in the morning, you will find that you are organised all day. Confusion

in the kitchen is a beginner's downfall. Be methodical. Tidy up as you go along. The breakfast plates can be warming, and everything that can be cooked in advance should be already cooked, so that you can greet your guests knowing that there is only a little last-minute preparation to be done.

Always wait on the tables quietly, with no clatter of dishes, and try to anticipate the needs of those being served. It is essential to be neatly dressed, with clean and tidy clothes, and special attention should be paid to one's hands, as they are seen by everyone. Any cuts on fingers need to be covered with a clean plaster. Those serving should never reach across anyone seated at the table in order to put down or remove a dish. Anything offered comes from the left-hand side, and soiled plates should be removed from the right-hand side.

When clearing the dining-room after the meal, stack the plates tidily in the kitchen or put them straight into the dishwasher. Keeping the decks clear avoids confusion, and that will wear you out quicker than anything else.

In a small guest house breakfast is usually at nine o'clock. If you wish to make it more flexible, have it from 8.45 a.m. until nine o'clock. It is wise to have the flexible quarter of an hour before you would really like them to eat, not after. Otherwise you will be serving breakfast until late morning, and be very late getting the tables cleared.

On Saturday, breakfast could be half an hour earlier than usual. This gives guests a chance to be out of their rooms by 10.30 a.m., enabling you to clean up before the next visitors arrive.

Buying and Storing Essentials

Always stock the basic ingredients for varying the breakfast main course, and, if you have a freezer, a supply of frozen fruit juices, sausages, vacuum packed fish, rolls, bread, croissants, potato cakes, butter and lemon sorbet will ensure that you always have something available for an unexpected guest. This, together with a well stocked store cupboard, will ensure that you never have to let late arrivals go hungry.

Eggs
If you buy little and often, you are unlikely to find any bad eggs. It is so annoying to find you have a pan full of fried eggs and the last one broken into it is bad! Eggs should be stored at room temperature to prevent yolks cracking. But in hot weather a suitable compromise is to keep the majority in the fridge and take out those you need for the next few days, keeping them in a dish or egg basket. Then they will be at room temperature when you need them. They should also be stored away from strong odours as they absorb them through their shells.

Bacon
Purchase fresh bacon regularly and keep it in the fridge. Its salt content does not make it very suitable for freezing. You may possibly find a grocer who will slice it for you. Then you will be able to select not only the cut you require, but the thickness of each slice. Many slaughterhouses will sell bacon direct to the public, so inquire locally, as it is much cheaper.

Kidneys
Kidneys do not keep very long, so they should be stored in the fridge and cooked the morning after purchase.

Sausages
You can use pork or beef sausages for breakfast and either will keep well in the freezer for one month. A butcher who makes his own quality sausages is well worth finding. It is not unknown for

guests to return home after their holidays laden down with sausages which taste so different to those from their own butcher! Experiment, too, and find a butcher whose sausages do not burst every time they begin cooking. You must have a good reliable sausage for the guests' breakfast!

Fish

Ask your fishmonger's advice and always buy really fresh fish. Most people in the Bed and Breakfast business who live by the sea or in a popular fishing area are invariably asked during the course of a fisherman's holiday to cook his latest catch for breakfast. So make sure that you are able to fillet a fish, and that you have a few recipes up your sleeve for the moment when there is a knock on the kitchen door, and your guest is standing there with his prize catch!

If you are worried about your own or your fishmonger's ability to fillet the fish correctly, the perfect solution is to keep, in the freezer, the commercial varieties of filleted kippers and other smoked fish. The most useful of these are those which come sealed in their own polythene bag, with butter already added. Although expensive, you can take them straight from the freezer, pop them into a pan of water, cook them for the required time, and the fish is ready. There are no lingering 'fishy' smells either. They also cook extremely well in a microwave oven, straight from the freezer.

Recipes and Hints

Many hotels now serve Continental breakfast only, and one of the attractions of a Bed and Breakfast holiday is the filling and nourishing breakfast which greets the visitor in the morning. This is especially welcomed by the many visitors from abroad who view it as part of the British holiday tradition.

Because holidaymakers often make do with a snack at lunchtime, a good breakfast provides sufficient energy to last until the evening meal. It is while on holiday, too, that people get a chance to eat a leisurely breakfast, which they usually have to rush, or even miss, during the rest of the year. A holiday is often the only time when people enjoy a cooked breakfast. Those who say they cannot stand more than a cup of tea in the morning are usually the first to complain if their holiday breakfast is not ample.

Add your own personal touches. Present each dish as well as possible and enhance the appearance of the food with colourful garnishes. Vary the menus according to the food in season and use local dishes as much as possible. Visitors will then have a taste of the cooking in your particular holiday area. A new variety of sausage or a different type of bread all contribute to the success of the holiday.

Breakfast Cereals
Have a selection of three or four different breakfast cereals on the table. This allows the guests to help themselves, and it is especially necessary when there are children, as it avoids wastage. Include a muesli or a cereal containing bran. Alternatively, put bran on the table separately as many people now add this to breakfast. A bowl of fresh fruit not only appeals to the eye but is popular with guests who like to add fruit to their cereal.

Bread
Do not serve toast the minute the guests appear in the dining-room. It should be brought in while they are eating their main course. If served too early, it will only become cold, hard and leathery by the time guests are ready for it. Serve it hot, in a toast rack, so that the pieces do not touch each other. This lets the steam escape and prevents the toast becoming soggy. When guests come down, have a selection of different breads on the table in a dish or basket. Vary the selection from day to day, but always have both white and wholemeal available. Try freshly warmed rolls or croissants for a change, and for slimmers put out a few crispbread. The important point to remember is to vary the selection and to have it all as fresh as possible. Your local baker will be only too pleased to tell you what he makes, and the guests will appreciate trying out the different fare.

Recipes for breads can be found in most recipe books, but it is useful to have one for Quick Breakfast Rolls. These can be prepared and cooked earlier in the morning, should you ever run out of bread completely.

Quick Breakfast Rolls
Take 1lb (450g) of self-raising flour (or 1lb (450g) plain flour and 2 tsp baking powder). Put flour into a bowl, add ½pt (275ml)

milk and one egg, and bind the mixture to a stiff dough. Shape into rolls, put on a floured tray and bake in a hot oven at 220°C (425°F) Mark 7 for 12–15 minutes.

Soda Bread
This uses up any milk which has soured, and is also delicious when sliced and fried the day after making, with eggs and bacon.

1lb (450g) plain white flour	*3 tsp baking powder*
1lb (450g) wholemeal flour	*Pinch of salt*
3 tsp sugar	*¾pt (450ml) sour milk or buttermilk*

Sift the flour, baking powder, salt and sugar into a bowl. Mix to a soft dough with the milk. Turn on to a floured board and shape (with floured hands) into an oblong loaf about 2in (5cm) high. Place on a greased baking sheet and bake at 200°C (400°F) Mark 6 for 40 minutes; or until the top is golden and the bottom sounds hollow when tapped.

Preserves
Honey and jam (especially apricot) are a very welcome change from marmalade at breakfast. So supplement the usual marmalade with occasional jars of these preserves. Buy or make as many home-made preserves as possible. They taste so much better.

For very busy people here is an ideal marmalade recipe. It needs very little supervision and the end result tastes delicious.

Uncle Jack's Marmalade
Put 12 oranges through the mincer and add the juice and pulp of 3 grapefruit. To each 1lb (450g) of fruit, add 2pt (1.25l) of water. Allow all this to lie in the preserving pan for 24 hours. Next day, bring it to the boil and boil for 45 minutes, but not galloping. Cool, and allow that to lie until the next day. To each 1pt (570ml) of liquid, allow 1½lb (675g) of warm preserving sugar. Boil liquid and sugar together for more than 1 hour, when it should set well.

Tea and Coffee
When guests come into the dining-room in the morning they will usually help themselves to cereal. This gives you a vital few

minutes in which to make the tea or coffee. The one thing guaranteed to upset holiday guests is starting off breakfast with a cup of tea which does not taste like the one they make at home. No two people pour their tea the same way. So the minute they come into the dining-room, take them a large pot of freshly made tea, and a pot of boiling water (remember to warm the teapot before adding the tea). Let the guests have as much tea as they want. Many guest houses only give one cup of tea at breakfast with guests having to ask for a top-up when they need one! Be generous and give each table a large pot. Use a good-quality tea which suits the local water, as that can alter the taste of many brands. Keep a few fruit teas in the store cupboard in case a guest prefers these. They will, no doubt, ask you if they do.

It is becoming increasingly popular to have coffee in the morning with breakfast, and Continental visitors will often prefer it. Be prepared for those guests and keep in a supply of good-quality coffee. The best results are obtained by using freshly ground coffee. This does not keep very long in large quantities, so if it is only occasionally asked for, buy it in the vacuum packs obtainable from most supermarkets or grocers. These store well unopened, and ensure that the flavour of the newly roasted bean is retained. Serve the coffee freshly made with hot (but not boiled) milk in a separate heated jug. Good-quality instant coffee should be available for guests as an alternative, and you can also keep a small jar of decaffeinated coffee for anyone who asks especially for that.

When you bring in the tea and coffee, ask if the guests would like a starter, and also find out their main course preference if you intend giving a choice. Although most of the food will be cooking already, you can finish its preparation while they eat their starter.

Starters

When guests come down in the morning they often do not feel like eating, so it is important to have an appetising starter. Offer a starter every morning, as well as the cereals already on the table, and again vary them as much as possible. Allow the guests to help themselves and, if practical, put the starter in a large bowl in the middle of the table, supply the guests with dishes and leave them to take as much as they would like. The extra minutes this saves, especially if you have no one to help you in the mornings, can be used by you to concentrate on the main course.

Fruit Juices

These include grapefruit, orange, pineapple and tomato. In season, it may be possible for you to serve them fresh by using a juice extractor. But during the rest of the year, use the frozen, tinned or carton varieties. The latter are especially useful as they store neatly in the fridge.

Yoghurt

The fruit varieties are most popular, but you can also serve plain yoghurt into which you stir thinly sliced fresh fruit in season, 1oz (25g) of chopped almonds or hazelnuts per portion and 1tsp of orange juice per portion. Buy yoghurt in as large quantities as possible, and serve in small individual dishes.

Melon

This is a good fresh starter when it is in season. Just cut into slices and serve each one on a small plate.

Stewed Apple

This can be prepared the previous night. Cook the apples in a little sugar until soft, and serve with brown sugar and a small jug of cream.

Dried Fruit Compôte

This can also be prepared in advance.

½lb (225g) dried fruit mixture, such as apricots, figs, apple rings
1pt (570ml) water

2–3oz (50–75g) demerara or Barbados sugar
A little lemon rind

Wash the fruit well and soak overnight in water. Add the lemon rind and sugar to the soaked fruit and the remaining water. Simmer until tender. Remove the lemon rind before serving.

Alternatively it can be cooked in a casserole in a low oven if that is more practical.

Prunes

These can be served, either hot or cold, with cream.

Porridge
This is popular on colder mornings. Serve with jugs of hot and cold milk; but it is especially delicious with syrup and cream.

Grapefruit
The tinned segments can be served as they are, or mixed with tinned mandarin oranges for an unusual fresh flavour.

If fresh grapefruit are reasonably priced, they can be served, either halved or in segments. If cutting into segments, remember to remove the pith, as this makes the fruit bitter, and save the juice in a dish underneath to serve with the segments. Fresh orange segments can also be added.

Half grapefruit are usually served with a cocktail cherry in the middle after easing out the segments with a grapefruit knife.

It is important to remember when serving fresh grapefruit never to put sugar on it. Leave it to the guests to add at the table to suit their own taste.

Orange or Lemon Sorbet
Many would not consider this when thinking of a starter for breakfast, but it is very popular. It is easily obtained in bulk from cash and carry suppliers, or you can make your own if you have a freezer. Serve it in ice-cream dishes, or scooped into empty orange or lemon skins, frosted in advance in the freezer. Here is Mary Norwak's recipe for Orange Sorbet.

2 tsp gelatine	*1 tsp grated orange rind*
½pt (275ml) water	*½pt (275ml) orange juice*
6oz (150g) sugar	*4 tbsp (25ml) lemon juice*
1 tsp grated lemon rind	*2 egg whites*

Soak the gelatine in a little of the water and boil the rest of the water and sugar for 10 minutes to a syrup. Stir the gelatine into syrup and cool. Add rinds and juices. Beat egg whites until stiff but not dry, and fold into the mixture. Freeze to a mush, beat once, then continue freezing, allowing 3 hours total freezing time. It will not go completely hard. Pack into containers and store in the freezer.

For lemon sorbet, use only lemon juice and rind instead of a mixture of orange and lemon.

Main Course Dishes

Many people starting Bed and Breakfast think that a traditional British bacon and egg breakfast is what is expected and continue to cook one for all the guests who arrive. But it is just as important to vary the main course for breakfast as it is to vary the starter. Guests will get fed up with the same thing every morning if they are staying with you for any length of time. And in terms of last-minute cooking, there is nothing quite like a large fried breakfast for inducing panic in the novice! It is all right if the family's egg yolks break in the frying pan, but can you serve it like that to a guest? It is not unknown in many guest houses for the family to be tucking into a huge fried egg omelette in the kitchen while the guests eat the only four eggs whose yolks did not break!

Easier Breakfast Dishes

There are many dishes which are much easier to cook than the traditional breakfast. They need less preparation, use less saucepans, and do not have you cooking so many things at once! They can also look most attractive if you garnish them well. Always have at least three items of food on the breakfast plate. It will then look much more appetising.

Poached Eggs
The eggs should be as fresh as possible, and at room temperature. If cooking in an egg poacher or a heavy saucepan, butter the poacher cups or the bottom of the pan well. This will not only prevent the eggs from sticking, it will also make the pan easier to clean afterwards. An average saucepan will poach four eggs. Use a wider pan for more eggs. Put about 1in (2.5cm) of water in the pan and bring it to simmering point. Break the eggs individually into a cup and slide them into the pan. Add no salt or vinegar as this makes the eggs tough and leathery. Simmer for 3 minutes and lift out of the pan with a perforated spoon. Serve straight away. Allow two eggs per person, unless they specifically ask for one.

Poached eggs can be served on toast, but remember to garnish it to look attractive with bacon rolls and tomato.

Bacon Rolls

Take rashers of freshly grilled back bacon and roll them. Secure with a cocktail stick. Alternatively, take rashers of back bacon, spread each with sausage-meat to within 1in (2.5cm) of the end. Roll them up, and place the rolls on a greased baking tin. Bake in a moderate oven for 20 minutes. This can be done first before any other cooking, and by the time you have done the poached eggs they will be ready to serve. Allow two bacon rolls per person.

Tomatoes

Halve the tomatoes round the waist, rather than from stem to tail. They cook and look better that way; they can also be cut into a water-lily shape. To do that you cut round the waist with a sharp knife in V shapes, then pull apart.

Tomatoes can be grilled or baked.

To grill, sprinkle the cut sides with black pepper, dried oregano and olive oil before grilling.

To bake, dot the cut sides with butter and black pepper and bake in a moderate oven for about 8 minutes.

Scrambled Eggs

Melt a small amount of butter in a heavy saucepan. The eggs cook more evenly if the pan is a heavy one. Mix 2 to 3 eggs per person with a little milk or single cream, and season to taste. Pour the eggs into the saucepan and stir gently with a wooden spoon over a low heat until the mixture is thick and creamy. Be sure to take the mixture away from the heat just before it has thoroughly cooked, as it will finish cooking in the pan—otherwise it may be tough and rubbery. Serve immediately. Scrambled eggs must be eaten as soon as they are cooked, so do not begin to cook until guests are eating their starter. They do not keep well and are apt to turn into a rather soggy mess if left in the pan too long.

The eggs can also be cooked in a bowl over a pan of boiling water. The result is a creamier dish which needs less looking after while cooking, and ensures easier washing up afterwards.

You can also add a spoonful of left-over white sauce to the scrambled eggs towards the end of cooking time, which makes it creamier. Garnish scrambled eggs with watercress, a ring of green pepper or parsley, and serve on toast with bacon rolls, tomatoes or sliced fried mushrooms.

Mushrooms
Wipe the mushrooms, slice and fry in a little butter or oil. Do not grill as they become too dry. Drain and serve.

Scrambled Eggs on Fried Bread
To avoid soggy toast, which can be the result of the eggs sitting too long on top of it, serve scrambled egg on a piece of fried bread instead. Lightly fry a thin slice of bread for about 2 minutes in hot oil, then drain on a paper towel to absorb excess grease. If cooked too slowly, the bread will become greasy. This is often a crisper base for scrambled eggs.

Savoury Scrambled Eggs
Finely chop several rashers of bacon and fry gently. Add a little chopped onion and cook until the onion is transparent. Add this to the beaten egg mixture and proceed as for scrambled eggs.

Piperade
The advantage of this variation on scrambled eggs is that the moisture from the pimentoes and onions makes it less likely to overcook and go dry.

1 onion, chopped	*8 large fresh eggs*
2 large pimentoes, chopped	*Butter for frying*
(tinned pimentoes will do)	*Salt and pepper*

Soften the chopped pimentoes and the onion by frying gently in the butter. Add the lightly beaten eggs and proceed as usual for scrambled eggs. Season with salt and pepper and garnish with chopped parsley. Add bacon rolls to the plate to complete the dish. Serves four.

Baked Eggs
The advantage of popping eggs into the oven is that it gives you time to prepare a second dish while the eggs are cooking.

To bake eggs, heat the oven to 180°C (350°F) Mark 4. Put a knob of butter into each individual ovenproof dish and put them in the oven to melt. When the butter has melted, break the eggs, one at a time, into the dishes. Season and put in the centre of the oven for 8–10 minutes. Serve one egg per person in the dish with toast at the side of the plate.

Alternatively, place chopped raw bacon in the bottom of the dish. Cook for 5 minutes until the fat has been released. Break in the eggs and bake for 8–10 minutes.

Coddled Eggs in Tomatoes

1 egg for each person	*Salt, pepper*
1 large tomato for each person	*½oz (15g) butter*

Cut off the top slice of tomato. Scoop out the pulp, (save for soups and sauces) and turn upside down to drain. Break an egg into each tomato, season and add a little butter on top. Bake in a moderate oven for 12–15 minutes until set. Serve with grilled bacon.

Fricassée of Eggs

This is an ideal dish for making eggs go further.

Chop hard-boiled eggs into a cheese sauce or plain white sauce, heat thoroughly and serve with croutons of fried bread and bacon rolls.

Remember to cool hard-boiled eggs in cold water to prevent the whites going dark and to make them easier to shell. Shelling large quantities of eggs is easier with your hands in a bowl of water, or under a running tap.

You can also use up cold gammon in the same way instead of hard-boiled eggs. Chop finely and add to a white or cheese sauce and serve on toast with chopped parsley as a garnish.

Hard-boiled Eggs and Cold Ham or Tongue

This is an ideal Saturday morning breakfast. There need be no panic, as it can all be prepared the night before. Served with sliced tomato, it often makes a pleasant change for guests to have a cold main course.

Mushrooms on Toast

Fry half a dozen mushrooms per person in butter. When browned, remove mushrooms and add black pepper and salt. Add flour to the butter in the pan, stir well, and add milk slowly to make a white sauce. Stir in the mushrooms. Serve on toast with a bacon roll on top.

Kidneys
Allow 1½ to 2 kidneys per person and use lamb's, calf's or pig's kidneys for breakfast.

Peel the outer membrane away before cooking and any white core also. Cut the kidney into slices and grill or fry.

To grill, brush over with fat or oil then grill for 10 minutes.

To fry, dip the kidneys in seasoned flour and fry in hot fat for 10 minutes. Serve with mushrooms and tomatoes.

Devilled Kidneys
Grill the kidneys, then spread them with a paste made up from 2oz (50g) butter flavoured to taste with chutney, dry mustard and curry powder, grill for one more minute. Serve with mushrooms.

Cheesy Rarebit on Toast

6oz (150g) grated Cheddar cheese	*Pinch salt*
2 tbsp (50ml) vinegar, beer or cider	*½–1 tsp mustard (according to taste)*
1oz (25g) butter	*Pinch black pepper*
	2 dsp (24ml) cream

Put all the ingredients in a pan; melt slowly, then spread them on hot buttered toast. Put under the grill to brown quickly on top. Serve with fried tomato or grilled bacon. Serves two.

Kippers
Prepare the fish for cooking by washing in cold water, then cut off the head, small fins and the tail. Kippers can be cooked in five different ways, depending on your convenience. Allow one pair per person.

To poach, put the fish in a frying pan or saucepan, cover with boiling water and poach gently for 5 minutes. This method is ideal if the kippers are salty.

To grill, dot with butter and put under a hot grill for 5 minutes.

To bake, butter the fish well, wrap in foil and bake in a hot oven at 200°C (400°F) Mark 6 for 15 to 20 minutes.

Another method which reduces the smell of the fish cooking is to pop them in a jug, cover them with boiling water and put a lid on the top. Leave for 5 minutes, pour off the water and finish cooking for a few minutes the way you prefer.

Kippers will also cook extremely well in a microwave oven. Follow the instructions in your recipe book.

Smoked Mackerel

These can be used instead of kippers. They are slightly richer in flavour and a little less strong. Cook as for kippers and serve seasoned with freshly ground pepper, and dotted with a knob of butter and a wedge of lemon.

Poached Egg on Haddock

Smoked haddock is often served for breakfast, usually poached in milk. There are two ways of presenting this dish, depending on how generous you want to be with the haddock. The first way is to serve a poached egg on a piece of poached smoked haddock, with toast at the side of the plate. Or poach the haddock, then flake it into a bowl (helping it to go further). Spread the flaked haddock on to squares of toast and pop a poached egg on top. Garnish with chopped parsley or paprika pepper.

Many people cannot eat fish in the morning as it repeats on them, so try if possible to serve fish together with an egg dish, for example kippers and scrambled eggs or poached egg on haddock, so that they can refuse the fish and just have the egg if they wish. Remember also to give the guests fish knives and forks, which makes the job of eating fish a lot easier, and put a large dish on the table for the disposal of any bones.

Kedgeree

This is an ideal dish for making a pound of fish go a long way!

Flake 1lb (450g) cooked smoked fish into a bowl. Add 2 chopped hard-boiled eggs, ¼pt (150ml) cream and ½lb (225g) cooked rice. Stir the mixture and season to taste with lemon juice, salt and cayenne pepper. Butter an ovenproof dish and spoon in the mixture. Cover and bake at 180°C (350°F) Mark 4 for 30 minutes. Garnish with parsley. Serves 6–8.

Baked Trout 1

Clean and bone the fish. Place in a greased ovenproof dish. Cover with seasoned flour and smother with lemon juice and butter. Cover and bake in a moderate oven for 20 minutes.

Herring can also be cooked the same way. It is a good idea to have a recipe like this ready when your fishermen guests return with their catches for breakfast!

Baked Trout 2
Place trout in an ovenproof dish. Cover with a mixture of half water, half malt vinegar. Bake in a moderate oven until the fish are cooked.

Fish Cakes
Mix mashed potato, cooked flaked white fish and chopped parsley together. Melt 1oz (25g) butter and mix this into the mixture. Add a beaten egg and salt and pepper to taste. Make into cakes, coat with egg and breadcrumbs and fry until golden brown. Serve with grilled tomato and a garnish of parsley and slices of lemon.

These will freeze very successfully. To freeze, cook, cool quickly and freeze. Reheat well from frozen in oven or re-fry before serving.

Boiled Eggs
There has been no mention so far of boiled eggs. This is because although the actual work involved is minimal, you may, after a while, consider it one of the most difficult dishes to cook! Recipe books are always telling you how to cook them, but the chances are that they will never turn out the way the guests like. More people complain about boiled eggs than anything else! The answer is always to ask the guests how many eggs they wish and how long they like their eggs cooked for.

Put the eggs (which should be at room temperature) into the simmering water and cook them for as long as they say. Rapid boiling will cause the shell to crack, and may also toughen the egg white.

When the eggs have been simmering for the required time, plunge them into a bowl of cold water for a few seconds to prevent further cooking, and serve.

More Difficult Breakfast Dishes

We come now to breakfast dishes which are more demanding of the cook. They cannot be left easily to cook themselves, and may require your undivided attention for a large part of the cooking time. They are difficult for beginners to cook in large numbers, but practice will make them considerably easier!

Omelettes

Once the basic mixture is made up, have two omelette pans or small frying pans on the go at the same time. Cook each omelette individually. Allow 2–3 eggs, salt, pepper and 1 tbsp (25ml) of cream, milk or water per person. Lightly whisk them all together and pour into the buttered pan. A medium to high heat is needed or they will go leathery. When golden brown on the underside and setting on the top, add the filling and fold over.
Savoury fillings include:

Tomato, skinned and chopped (to skin tomatoes, cover with boiling water, leave for approximately 1 minute, remove and they will skin easily)
Bacon, cooked and chopped
Smoked fish, cooked and flaked
Kidney, cooked and chopped
Mushrooms, cooked and chopped (small button mushrooms will not discolour the omelette so much)
Chopped cold ham
Grated cheese
A mixture of bacon and cooked potato
A mixture of chopped ham and cooked onion

Serve each omelette with a little of the savoury filling on top.
Alternatively, chopped ham, grated cheese or a mixture of fresh herbs can be added to the basic recipe and cooked with the eggs. Garnish with parsley or tomato for added colour.

Stuffed Tomatoes

4 large tomatoes (one for each person)	*1 tbsp (25g) chopped bacon or ham*
2 tbsp (50g) breadcrumbs	*½ tsp chopped parsley*
1 tsp finely chopped onion	*½ tsp tomato pulp, or*
Grated cheese	*sauce*

Cut small slices from the top of the tomatoes and scoop out the pulp. Turn upside down to drain. Cook the onion in a little oil. When cooked, add the other ingredients. Cook gently for a further 2 minutes. Fill the tomatoes with the stuffing and sprinkle a little grated cheese on top. Bake in a moderate oven for 15 minutes. Serve on rounds of fried bread.

Stuffed Pancakes
Make a plain pancake batter keeping to the following proportions:

4oz (100g) plain flour   *1 egg*
Salt and pepper   *½pt (275ml) milk*

Leave for at least 30 minutes. Fry each pancake in a little oil or fat. When cooked keep warm until the filling is prepared.

Mushroom filling. Wipe and slice ½lb (225g) mushrooms, cook in a little butter until tender. Add ½ tsp flour, 2 tbsp (50ml) cream and season with salt, pepper and nutmeg. Fill pancakes with mixture, roll up and serve with sausages.

Smoked fish filling. Bind ½lb (225g) flaked smoked fish in a white sauce with chopped parsley and salt and pepper. Fill the pancakes, roll up and serve with tomatoes as a garnish.

The unfilled pancakes, once cooked, freeze well. Cool and place a layer of greaseproof paper between each before stacking and freezing in polythene or a plastic box. To reheat, separate while frozen, thaw at room temperature and either cover with foil and heat in a low oven, or cover with a cloth and heat on a plate over a steaming saucepan.

Savoury Pancakes
These are useful if short of eggs, but with bits and pieces to use up. They are similar to drop scones in consistency and can be cooked individually or as one large pancake and then cut into six or eight to serve. Basic mixture for 6 individual pancakes is:

2 eggs   *¼pt (150ml) milk*
4oz (100g) plain flour   *Salt and pepper*

Add the beaten eggs to the flour and seasoning. Pour in milk slowly. Mix well. To this mixture you can add: (1) three rashers chopped bacon and one small, chopped onion precooked in a little oil and drained; or (2) 4oz (100g) of sausage meat well mixed into the batter; or (3) the drained contents of a small can of sweetcorn. Serve the pancakes with mushrooms and grilled tomatoes.

Sausages
Sausages take longer to cook than most other breakfast foods. They must have 15 to 20 minutes' cooking to ensure they are

cooked right through. Slow cooking will also help to keep their skins intact. Pricking the skins may work, but it is not guaranteed! They need to be fried, as they brown better than when grilled or baked. A good tip before putting them in the frying pan is to roll them lightly in flour. This seals in the juices and gives a better taste.

Allow two sausages per person and serve with scrambled egg and grilled tomato. A little fried onion or fried apple rings provide an unusual garnish.

They can also be served with baked beans and round chips, or potato cakes.

Round Chips
Parboil potatoes for 10 minutes. Cut into round slices and fry in hot fat, as for chips.

Potato Cakes

1lb (450g) mashed cooked potato	*1 egg*
	Milk
Salt and pepper	*3oz (75g) grated cheese,*
¼–½ tsp mustard (accord-	*ham, cooked bacon or*
ing to taste)	*cooked flaked fish*

Beat the potato to remove the lumps. Add salt and pepper, beaten egg, flavouring and milk if necessary. Mix well and shape into cakes on a floured board. Fry quickly on both sides in hot fat or oil, then more slowly until hot all the way through.

Bacon
Grill the bacon if possible, as this allows a lot of excess fat to drain away. It also frees the frying pan for other things. Use back, middle or streaky rashers, depending on your budget. Arrange them slightly overlapping on the rack of the grill with the rinds exposed to the heat. This bastes and flavours the lean bacon underneath. Cook slowly at first while the fat is melting, then hotter until the fat is transparent. Do be careful though, that the bacon does not burn. It has a tendency to do this under the grill.

If cooking bacon rashers which have been frozen, pat them dry first with kitchen towel to absorb excess moisture. Allow two rashers per person. Bacon is such a versatile food that it can be served with almost every other breakfast dish.

French Bread
Soak slices of bread in beaten egg and fry lightly and quickly in oil, until crispy. Serve with bacon and sausages.

Kidneys Rolled in Bacon
Roll each prepared kidney in a rasher of bacon. Fasten with a skewer and grill slowly for approximately 10 minutes until cooked. There is no need to baste as the bacon fat will do that. Serve with grilled tomatoes.

Fried Eggs
If planning a bacon, sausage, tomato, fried bread and egg breakfast, leave the cooking of the eggs until the guests are almost ready for their main course. The rest can be cooked in advance and kept warm in the oven, but the eggs will spoil. To cook a successful fried egg always make sure that you start off with a clean pan and clean cooking oil, otherwise you will end up with a messy egg. Heat a little oil in a frying pan. When hot slide the egg carefully into the pan to prevent the yolk from breaking. Cook very gently, basting from time to time with the hot fat until the top is set. (Or if you are too busy to baste the eggs, cover the pan with a lid. It works just as well.) Do not attempt to turn the egg over, as you will end up with a pan full of runny broken yolks! Lift the egg out of the pan with a fish slice and serve immediately.

To give an idea of how you can vary the breakfast menu here are menus for seven days, using some of the dishes mentioned. Flexibility is the most important thing. Guests will all have their likes and dislikes, so let them know that you will try to please them, for example by doing a boiled egg if they do not wish a large cooked breakfast that morning.

Day One
  A traditional British Breakfast
  Grapefruit and cereals (An acid starter such as grapefruit counteracts the fattiness of the fried breakfast to follow.)
  Egg, bacon, sausage, tomato and fried bread
  Toast and preserves
This is a difficult breakfast to cook, but if guests are staying for a week, it is a good idea to impress them early in their holiday.

Towards the end of the week they will usually want a lighter breakfast as they are beginning to fill up with the extra holiday food!

Day Two
Lemon sorbet and cereals
Filleted smoked haddock, flaked on to buttered toast and served with a poached egg on top
   Or
Poached egg on toast with fried tomato, for guests who do not want the fish
Croissants or hot rolls (when the main course dish includes toast, serve other hot breads)

Day Three
Dried fruit compôte and cereals
Fried sausages, baked beans and potato cakes
   Or
Boiled eggs
Toast, honey and marmalade

Day Four
Fruit juices and cereals
Kippers and scrambled egg
   Or
Scrambled egg on toast, garnished
Hot rolls

Day Five
Melon and cereals
Kidneys, bacon, mushrooms and fried bread
   Or
Boiled eggs
Croissants and toast

Day Six
Yoghurt and cereals
Scrambled egg on toast, bacon rolls and grilled tomatoes
   Or
Baked egg
Hot rolls and toast

Day Seven
Porridge (on cold mornings) or fruit juice and cereals
Cold ham or tongue, hard-boiled egg and tomato
  Or
Boiled eggs
Toast

Children's Breakfasts

It is much better to check before cooking for a child that they like whatever is planned for breakfast. This will avoid wastage. Parents will usually give you a good idea what will or will not be eaten, but it will help if you know of a few children's dishes for the days when there may be nothing else preferred. Serve a poached egg on baked beans or spaghetti. Chop up sausages into scrambled egg. Serve fish fingers, baked beans and round chips. A layer of jam or marmalade on fingers of French bread will almost always be eaten.

For the very youngest you could keep a jar or two of baby food in the store cupboard. This will be welcomed by parents who may have arrived too late in the evening to buy their own in time for breakfast next day.

Special Diets

Trust the guest to advise you should they have any special dietary requirements. They will usually have done this in their letter confirming their holiday arrangements. Diabetics will often bring their own food, and vegetarians too will give you advice on how you can adapt a breakfast dish to cater for their needs.

If you consider your guests as individuals, and take an interest in them, you will find yourself going out of your way to make them feel welcome.

7

The Guests Themselves

What do you do when the guests arrive?
Most people in the Bed and Breakfast business remember their first guests very well. They are rather important! However, do not let yourself be carried away and rush out to greet them, announcing that they are the first arrivals. You must look as though you have been taking in paying guests for years! They may have worked very hard indeed saving for this holiday and a novice landlord or landlady greeting them at the front step could make them wonder if it is money well spent! You will obviously gain more confidence as each guest comes and goes, and hopefully acquire a great deal of expertise in putting them at their ease.

When guests do arrive, often at the end of a long tiring journey, settle them down with a cup of tea, or even a welcoming glass of sherry if you like. It is most important then to show them round the house. Let them see the dining-room, lounge, bathroom, etc., as well as their bedroom accommodation. When this is forgotten visitors do not feel so relaxed. Even if they have a brochure, remind them of the mealtimes, and if no tea-making facilities are provided, find out if they would like early morning tea. This initial chat and necessary introductions are important to the success of the holiday. You are both eyeing each other up!

They want to see what kind of person you are, and vice versa. A pleasant manner on arrival will soon dispel any fears they may have.

What do you do about keys?
Once a guest has moved into a room, it becomes their room for the duration of their stay. It is only courtesy that you knock on the door before entering, and never show other people over the room if they have come to see the house. If you provide all the guests with keys, both to their rooms and the front door, they will feel free to come and go as they wish. Keep master or duplicate keys yourself so that you can go in and clean the rooms during the day if they are out.

Should there be any restrictions and rules?
Although difficult to do when just beginning to take in guests because you are accustomed to the house to yourself, have as few restrictive notices as possible. The guests do not like them. Guest houses where you have to return by 10 o'clock every night and baths are on Sundays only do not encourage return visitors! The question of 'no smoking' in bedrooms, however, is more difficult. Many guest houses now restrict smoking to public rooms only and display notices to this effect. But it is probably true to say that people will either continue smoking despite a

notice or move to another guest house. All one can hope to do is provide adequate ashtrays and have sensible fire precautions.

The majority of guests, thankfully, are very aware of being in someone else's home and treat it with respect.

Should guests use the telephone?
It is possible to install a pay phone for guests' use, but the additional rental may outweigh any advantages. Guests will usually pay for the calls they make, often by going through the operator to inquire about the charge. In a town, let guests know where the nearest kiosk is situated.

What do you do about washing, ironing and drying facilities?
Remembering that a great many visitors to Bed and Breakfast accommodation are tourists, there is likely to be a need to wash and dry clothes while travelling. Also families with young babies welcome somewhere to wash and dry nappies regularly. Any provision made towards providing them with access to a sink, spin dryer and clothes line will be very welcome.

Should you allow guests to use the garden?
The garden and any other facilities in your home should be shared with the guests whenever you feel able to do so. Flexibility is the key to having guests. If you are prepared to be sympathetic towards guests and their needs, you will get much more feedback from them. Many a guest house boasts a beautiful garden because gardening guests have been allowed to exercise their green fingers while on holiday!

What should you do if prospective guests want to see the house before they book?
Many small guest-house owners find this difficult to do, as there is always the possibility of no booking forthcoming. You are likely to feel that when a guest rejects the house that they are also rejecting a part of yourself, and you have to become hardened a little towards that.

It has been known for one lady to view a house throughout, then to declare that, no, Henry her poodle would not be happy there, so she did not think she would like it either! But do be willing to show anyone round the house (apart from bedrooms which are occupied by guests at that time. You can in those circumstances perhaps show them yours, explaining that it is similar to a guest room etc.).

Can guests look in the kitchen?

There is no requirement that the food preparation area be open to public access. However, discouraging or refusing to allow a guest in, should they ask, may indicate that you have something to hide! This is another good reason for keeping the kitchen tidy and well organised.

Should you offer guests breakfast in bed?

You can offer guests a Continental breakfast in bed, consisting of croissants or rolls, butter, preserves, tea or coffee. However, unless you have help and it is served earlier than the conventional breakfast, you are likely to be very rushed.

What do you do should a guest cancel a booking?

When a guest cancels a booking at very short notice, or does not turn up at all, you are entitled to claim compensation for loss of business. You should, however, try to re-let if possible. The amount claimed from the guest is usually the cost of the proposed stay less the costs which were not incurred on food, electricity, heating, etc.

Write in the first instance to the guests involved asking for payment and reminding them of their obligations. If this is not successful, you have to weigh up the loss involved against the costs of recovering the money through court action.

Fortunately, it is a very rare occurrence, but should it happen to you and you need further advice, go along and see the Trading Standards or Consumer Protection Officer.

Do you have any special problems if you live on a farm?

To many visitors, a farm holiday is ideal. They get all the pleasures of the country with none of the responsibility and as much of the hard work as they care to do. If willing, they often get roped in to help with the seasonal jobs and quite literally 'make hay while the sun shines'. For town visitors, much can be learned about farming, and for children especially it is often their first glimpse of real farm animals.

However, farm buildings, yards and fields often appear to be playgrounds for children, and guests and their families must be made aware of their dangers.

Your children may have grown up on the farm and know the dangers and areas to avoid and you may at first forget that town children do not have the same awareness. The Health and Safety Executive (address in Appendix B) will supply leaflets on agricultural safety for children and the prevention of accidents. These should be left around prominently for guests. The Agricultural Development and Advisory Service of the Ministry of Agriculture, Fisheries and Food will also advise on the provision of farm accommodation for guests, and how to help them appreciate their holiday.

What do you do if guests want to bring their dog?
First, ascertain its size. There is a lot of difference between a great dane coming to stay and a corgi! If too large for your house say no. On arrival they usually stay in either the owner's bedroom or car, as they should not be allowed in the lounge or dining room where they may upset other guests. Ask the owner to bring a basket or blanket for the dog to sleep on and whether they are going to take responsibility for feeding. When they do so, it is not usual to make a charge. But if they would like you to feed the dog, then you should charge enough to cover the cost of food and time involved.

What do you do if the dogs eat the guests' meat?
It has been known to happen! Whatever you do, do not panic. Tell the guests what has happened and why their meal may be a little later than usual. If there is no food in the house, take them all to the nearest restaurant and treat them to a meal out. If they are allowed to share such experiences with you, you will be able to laugh about it together. When other crises arise, and everyone has a few, do not worry. Guests almost always help out once they know what has gone wrong.

How much do you charge for children?
For children under two, you would charge only a nominal amount, say one-sixth of the nightly charge, to cover the costs of providing a cot, sheets and perhaps some food. For children aged between two and eleven, half the adult price is reasonable, for those aged between eleven and thirteen, three-quarters.

How do you cope when children or pets become really annoying?
Both children and pets have one thing in common. They
themselves are usually no trouble. It is the parents or owners
who create the problems! Although you have turned the house
over to the guests, it is still your home, and you have the comfort
of any other guests to consider. So do not put up with anything
which for you is unreasonable. If a child wakes in the middle of
the night and is crying in the corridor, do not leave it crying if
the parents do not hear. Attend to it, put it back in its room, and
possibly have a word with the parents in the morning. Suffering
too much in silence may upset you and mean discomfort for
other guests. You have to set the standard of behaviour.

What do you do if a guest is ill?
Occasionally a guest on holiday with you takes ill. If they need a
doctor, phone your own general practitioner, who will either ask
them to come to the surgery or will call and see the guest. The
patient will simply be asked to fill in a temporary resident form.

A good first-aid kit should be kept for any emergencies, and
common sense and a basic knowledge of first aid usually help you
to cope with any eventuality. You will also find that other guests
are more than willing to lend a hand in a crisis.

For visitors confined to bed, do not just leave them alone in
your home with no care. Check they are all right throughout the
day, making tea and coffee if necessary. And arrange an attractive
tray, possibly with a small flower vase on it, so that they can have
meals in the bedroom.

What do you do if a guest dies?
Although, fortunately, it does not happen often, some guidance
about a death in the house will help you cope. Above all, stay
calm and avoid upsetting the other guests. Your reserves of tact
and ingenuity are likely to be taxed to their fullest extent! Phone
your GP straight away. He will give you further advice. If he has
not been treating the guest previously, it will be necessary for
him to inform the local coroner. Also telephone the local police
station, who will need to send someone round. Until they arrive
do not move the body. If necessary, it can be covered up with a
blanket.

How do you cope when you desperately need a break?
Most people in the Bed and Breakfast trade, because they are
meeting guests very intensively for a large part of the day, need a
safety valve when things begin to get on their nerves. It will
almost certainly happen from time to time. Everyone develops
their own way of escape. For some it may be going out for
Sunday dinner and having a meal cooked for them. Others have a
friend who comes in to help on occasional evenings; just having
someone else to talk to, especially if that week's guests are
difficult to live with, can alleviate some of the tension. Even
sitting down in the middle of a rough week and counting the
money can do wonders for your morale and remind you of one
of the reasons you are taking in guests!

When are you most likely to get complaints?
Complaints, if there are going to be any, usually come within the
first few days of guests' arrival in the house. This is when they
find that things are not quite as they expected. They are still
likely to be tired and have not usually begun to relax. This is one
of the reasons why a friendly and helpful welcome settles them
down very quickly.

Which guests are most irritating?
Doing Bed and Breakfast will very rapidly develop any skills you
have in dealing with people. You have to be able to keep on being
pleasant, even though you cannot stand that particular person!
The most irritating guests from the host's point of view are those
who become too demanding, trying to gain attention more often
than necessary. They do not leave you with enough time to
devote to the others. They may even come and sit in the kitchen
while the cook is trying to prepare a meal. Tact and persistence
on your part will be necessary.

How do you cope with guests whose attitudes differ from yours?
Although you set the standards by your personal standards and
values and the way you live with your family, you have to adjust
constantly to others; over the years you are likely to find that
your guests have changed your attitudes to many things—both
by their conversation and by the constant questioning of one's
own attitudes which happens when living so closely with other
people. You become more tolerant. When you start you are likely

to feel most comfortable with those guests whose views are similar to your own. You will know what to expect from them. The rules by which they live will be similar to yours. However, a close relationship between yourself and the guests offers both parties a chance to learn a lot more about each other. This is especially true when many visitors are from overseas. One study of tourists and their hosts in Bed and Breakfast accommodation found that one of the biggest problems for landlords and landladies was learning to accept the values and expectations of various nationalities. These are often very different from our own. Overseas guests usually stay in Bed and Breakfast houses in order to learn more about the people and the country's customs and way of life. But by sharing experiences with each other you are likely to have learned much more about them by the time they leave.

When do you present the bill?
If staying for a week or longer guests will usually inquire when you would like to be paid. Often those paying cash would prefer to pay at the beginning of the week. Then they do not have to worry about losing the money. If accepting payment by cheque (not accompanied by a cheque card), Wednesday is a convenient day, as this gives you a chance to clear it at the bank before guests leave on Saturday. Otherwise Friday evening is the usual time for settlement of bills. Always give a receipt.

What do you do when guests leave?
It is very important to spare the time to say goodbye. Do not let them leave feeling you are no longer interested in them once they have paid their bill! Guests whose company you have enjoyed you will often feel genuinely sorry to see go. For those who number among the least popular, make a good pretence of looking sorry!

If guests have enjoyed their stay with you, the most appropriate way for them to record their comments is in a Visitors' Book. No Bed and Breakfast establishment should be without one, and it should be bought in good time for the first guests' arrival. Allow the guests to write whatever they like in it. You may get poems, drawings, photos, kind comments and rude ones. But there is nothing quite like it for reading during the long cold winter evenings, and spending a few hours bringing back warm, happy memories or otherwise! It serves as a good reminder of those guests you would like to see again. They will have conveniently provided their names and addresses, and at Christmas next year's brochure can be tucked inside a Christmas card!

The longer you are in the Bed and Breakfast business, the more you will realise that the guests who come back most often are the ones who are most like yourself. The ones who enjoy their stay will write back and re-book year after year. They will also recommend friends who will enjoy your company.

How do you improve the business?
Beginning in a small way, the guests will teach you their needs as you progress. Re-invest some of the profit to improve facilities next year, for example putting in more hand-basins the following year, central heating, etc.

Aim for good quality from the outset, never falling below the standard you set yourself. The competition is so keen nowadays that if you do not keep up a high standard, you will soon go out of business. Visitors like to feel they are getting more than value for their money. If your standards are too low, your business will be the one to be dropped. Experience is the best teacher, though, and each year, as your standards rise, running the business will become a lot easier!

What are the main disadvantages?
The answer which comes most readily to mind is exhaustion! You do get very tired working, often without a break, for eight to twelve weeks in the summer. Also your home is not your own for that time, and you cannot just pack up and go away for the weekend. It is not always easy, too, especially in the beginning, to give as much attention as you would like to your own family. Sometimes they do have to come second, the guests' needs always taking priority.

What are the main advantages?
These obviously far outweigh the disadvantages, otherwise people would not continue for so long. For them it is something which obviously gives them a great deal of enjoyment. The financial side is very important. One can buy things for one's own family which would not otherwise have been possible. But

most people would rather emphasise the pleasure in giving someone a happy holiday, getting a clean plate at the end of a meal and the new outlook which comes from meeting people from all walks of life. You make friends, and share fun and laughter together. However exhausted you feel at the end of the year, there are plenty of happy memories to encourage you on to the next.

'Tired and thin we struggled in,
Happy and stout we waggled out.'

'We know you love us really, so stop sending us home.'

'Thank you for the homeliness, friendliness and the freedom.'

'Looking forward to many, happy returns.'

'Lovely grub
Roll on next year.'

Appendix A

Minimum Standards

Minimum Requirements for the Physically Handicapped

At least one entrance must have no steps or be equipped with a ramp whose gradient does not exceed 1:12.

All doors (including those of WCs, private bathroom etc.) must have at least 74cm (29in) clear opening width, with head-on approach.

All essential accommodation, if not on the ground floor, must be served by an adequately sized lift.

All lifts must have gate opening of at least 74cm (29in); lifts must be at least 122cm (48in) deep and 91cm (36in) wide.

At least one bedroom and one public WC must be suitable for the disabled.

In bedrooms, private or public bathrooms and WCs used by the disabled, the clearance around beds, and to reach wash-basins, WCs etc. must be at least 74cm (29in) and there must be turning space of 122cm (48in) by 122cm (48in).

The English Tourist Board Minimum Standards for Serviced Accommodation

Bedrooms

Reasonable free space for movement and for easy access to beds, doors and drawers. Minimum floor areas, excluding private bath or shower areas: single bedrooms 60 sq ft (5.60 sq metres); double bedrooms 90 sq ft (8.40 sq metres); twin-bedded rooms 110 sq ft (10.20 sq metres); family rooms 30 sq ft (2.80 sq metres) plus 60 sq ft (5.60 sq metres) for each double bed, and/or 40 sq ft (3.70 sq metres) for each single adult bed and/or 20 sq ft (1.85 sq metres) for each cot.

Minimum bed sizes (except children's beds): single beds 6ft × 2ft 6in (183 × 76cm); double beds 6ft × 4ft (183 × 122cm); spring interior, foam or similar quality mattresses in sound condition; bedding clean and in sufficient quantity.

Beds made daily. Linen changed at least weekly and for every new guest. Soap and clean towel for every new guest—replenished or changed as required. All bedrooms to have dressing-table or equivalent and mirror; wardrobe or clothes hanging space with four hangers per person; adequate drawer space; bedside table or equivalent, one chair or equivalent; waste-paper container, ashtray, bedside rugs or mats where no carpet; at least one window and adequate ventilation, opaque curtains or blinds on all windows; adequate heating according to season. Minimum lighting levels: single bedrooms 100 watts or equivalent; double bedrooms 150 watts or equivalent.

Bathrooms
At least one bathroom, with bath or shower, available for guests at all reasonable times. Hot water at all reasonable times. No extra charge for baths or showers.

WCs
At least one WC equipped with toilet paper and disposal bin for guests' use.

General
Establishment clean throughout; all decorations, furnishings, floor coverings and fittings in good condition.

For Service and Public Rooms
Bed-making and room cleaning service. Breakfast room (unless served in bedrooms). Public areas adequately lit for safety and comfort. Guests informed when booking if access to establishment restricted during day. Adequate heating according to season.

Appendix B

Useful Addresses

Ministry of Agriculture, Fisheries and Food, Whitehall Place, London SW1. For your local office, see 'Agriculture, Fisheries and Food, Ministry of—' in the telephone book. The Agricultural Development and Advisory Service of the Ministry of Agriculture (ADAS) produce a paper on farmhouse and self-catering accommodation on the farm. This is available from your local Ministry of Agriculture office or from Ministry of Agriculture, Fisheries and Food (Publications), Tolcarne Drive, Pinner, Middlesex HA5 2DT.

Council for Small Industries in Rural Areas (COSIRA). Information on loans can be obtained from Director of Credit Services and Loans, COSIRA, 141 Castle Street, Salisbury, Wilts. SP1 3TP or your local COSIRA office.

English Tourist Board, 4 Grosvenor Gardens, London SW1W 0DU.

Scottish Tourist Board, 23 Ravelston Terrace, Edinburgh EH4 3EU.

Wales Tourist Board, Brunel House, 2 Fitzalan Road, Cardiff CF2 1UY.

Northern Ireland Tourist Board, River House, 48 High Street, Belfast BT1 2DS.
Each Tourist Board may also be able to provide information on starting in the Bed and Breakfast business.

Holiday Care Service, 2 Old Bank Chambers, Station Road, Horley, Surrey RH6 9HW.

The Royal Association for Disability and Rehabilitation (RADAR), 25 Mortimer Street, London W1N 8AB. They are always pleased to advise on any particular problems.

Disabled Living Foundation, 346 Kensington High Street, London W14 8NS. They will advise on the suitability of equipment for disabled people and will also help you find a suitable architect should you wish to alter your premises.

Health and Safety Executive, Baynards House, 1 Chepstow Place, London W2 4TF.

Local offices of HM Agricultural Inspectorate will also supply further information on agricultural safety.

Royal Society for the Prevention of Accidents, Cannon House, The Priory, Queensway, Birmingham B4 6BS.

Bed and Breakfast Guides

Bed and Breakfast Guide, The Ramblers' Association, 1–5 Wandsworth Road, London SW8 2LJ. Tel. 01-582-6878

Bed and Breakfast in Britain, Herald Advisory Services, 23a Brighton Road, South Croydon, Surrey CR2 6UE. Tel. 01-681-3595

Bed and Breakfast Stops and *The Farm Holiday Guide*, Farm Holiday Guides Ltd, 18 High Street, Paisley, Scotland PA1 2BX. Tel. 041-887-0428

Bed, Breakfast and Evening Meal, Pastime Publications Ltd, 7 Royal Terrace, Edinburgh EH7 5AB. Tel. 031-556-0057

Farm House Holidays, 14 High Street, Godalming, Surrey GU7 1ED. Tel. 04868-28525

Fire Rules

FIRE ACTION

Visitors are advised to familiarise themselves with the fire routine for these premises which is given below:—

If you discover a fire

Operate the nearest fire alarm point. These points are sited

On hearing the alarm

(The sound of the alarm is:—

Ensure that others in the immediate vicinity are awake.

Do not stop to dress fully but if possible put on a dressing gown (or coat) and shoes.

Go to . . . .
which is the place of assembly, shutting all doors behind you.

Do not stop to collect personal belongings.

Do not use lifts.

Act calmly.

Should the normal exit route be affected by fire, follow the alternative "FIRE EXIT" signs which will lead you to a place of safety.

(Note: This item should not be included where the premises has only one escape route.)

Do NOT re-enter the premises until given the all-clear to do so by a person in authority.

(Note: Small fires may be tackled with the fire equipment provided but only if it is safe to do so.)

Appendix D

A Typical Insurance Policy

The Standard Policy covers

Trade Contents

Furniture, furnishings, decorations, fittings, stock in trade and all other contents are insured against fire, theft, explosion, storm, flood and many other perils.

Glass

Cover against breakage of fixed glass and mirrors including boarding-up costs, and making good damage to window frames. Washbasins and other sanitary fittings are also insured.

Loss of Income

Insurance for either 12 or 24 months against loss of income resulting from trading being interrupted or even totally suspended by damage covered under the Trade Contents and Glass sections.

Money

Insurance of money (including NHI stamps) against loss from theft, hold-up or other causes not only from the business premises, but also from the insured's home, a bank night safe or whilst in transit.

Criminal Assault

Substantial benefits for death or disablement of the insured or employees including payment for damage to clothing and personal effects.

Legal Liability

Cover against liability to employees, guests and the general public for accidental injury or damage arising in connection with the business, which includes liability arising from defects in goods sold or supplied and liability for guests' property.

Optional covers are available for

Buildings

If you own or are responsible for insuring the buildings, these can be covered against the same perils as the Trade Contents.

Refrigerated Stock

Insurance against deterioration of cold stocks caused by accidental failure of plant or electricity supply or leakage of refrigerant.

Accidental Damage

'All Risks' cover for: cash registers, automatic vending and amusement machines and office machinery; televisions, aerials and accessories; neon and other illuminated signs.

Guests' Effects

Legal liability for loss or damage to guests' effects is covered under the standard policy. If you wish to offer compensation even when no legal obligation exists, extended cover is available under the Trade Contents section.

Index